A STORY of
SUFFERING
and HOPE

A STORY of SUFFERING and HOPE

Lessons from Latino Youth

Eileen McNerney, CSJ

Paulist Press
New York/Mahwah, N.J.

Cover design by Sharyn Banks
Book design by Lynn Else

Library of Congress Cataloging-in-Publication Data

McNerney, Eileen.
    A story of suffering and hope : lessons from Latino youth / Eileen McNerney.
        p. cm.
    Includes bibliographical references
    ISBN 0-8091-4343-7 (alk. paper)
    1. McNerney, Eileen. 2. Church work with youth—Catholic Church. 3. Church work with Hispanic Americans. I. Title.

BX4705.M2538A3 2005
267'.62279496'08968073—dc22

2005001958

Published by Paulist Press
997 Macarthur Boulevard
Mahwah, New Jersey 07430

www.paulistpress.com

Printed and bound in the
United States of America

CONTENTS

CONTENTS

Contents

ACKNOWLEDGMENTS

I am grateful to a number of people who have had a hand in shaping this book: to Anne Joujon-Roche Kestle who first coaxed me into the writing process and the Mesa Refuge program which gave me the opportunity to lay down the first lines; to my earliest readers, Louise Ann Micek, CSJ, Lorraine Thibault, CSJ, Judith Wemmer, CSJ, Christine Ray, CSJ, Maureen Habel, Dana Mildebrath, Christa Sheehan, Corrine Bayley, and Father William P. McLaughlin for their feedback and encouragement; to Jessica Clark and Jay Martin who buoyed my confidence and guided my editing efforts; and to Serafin Serrano, Arturo Guerrero, and Roberto Gonzalez, who assured me that I was faithful to a complex and unfolding story.

DEDICATION

To the young people of Santa Ana, who,
caught between two cultures,
build their strength by walking and teach me how to love.

*The place God calls you to is the place where your deep gladness
and the world's deep hunger meet.*
Frederick Buechner

X-rays aren't strong enough to detect my broken spirit.
J. David Lopez (20)

AUTHOR'S NOTE

Every day I walk into a culture that is very different from my own. It is the world where first and second generation immigrants from Mexico and Central America dwell in poverty in the land of plenty. In this hardscrabble world, I find dark corners where hopeless youth live. I don't always understand what I see. Sometimes I think that I am here to bear witness to the tragedy of a generation of young people who are dying from within while never giving life a chance. If I have any understanding at all of this dark world, it is because the young people at Taller San Jose tell me their stories and let me see through their eyes. But it isn't easy to see the world as they do. The students and I—we grew up very differently.

I was raised Irish Catholic in a stable family environment where education and upward mobility were primary values. I am American from my birth and to separate myself from my learned values would be akin to stripping away my own skin. It's hard to describe *American*, even to oneself, but I know that I am hard-working, independent, resourceful, and filled with optimism. I have also become used to convenience, cleanliness, variety, and the *new*, whatever it is and wherever it can be found. I pay attention to my world, but I haven't always viewed myself as a world citizen. Mostly, I'm a self-reliant American.

The young people that I work with straddle an uncomfortable bridge between Hispanic and American cultures. Most believe themselves to be Mexican, but if they return to Mexico, and some have never been there, the real Mexicans would label them *pochos*. *Pochos* are hybrids of sorts. They no longer speak español pura. Their first language has been bastardized by the long, strong influence of the border. Pochos don't even walk Mexican anymore; they carry the energy in their bodies differently now, though they probably don't know that they do so. They have lost a sensitivity to subtle social norms that predominate south of the border. Some of these young people visit family in Mexico and, while they love Mexico, they are also restless to get back home to California. But these young pochos aren't really American either. Americans criticize their work ethic, their easy willingness to subjugate their personal progress to the transient needs of friends and family, their seeming passivity, and their perceived pessimism.

These young people get lost between two cultures. Most of them have been raised in chronic, crushing poverty. If they don't know how poor they are, it's only because they see around them people poorer than themselves. They're always worried about rent and food—survival issues. They share housing with many extended family members and some hangers-on who have nowhere else to lay out a bedroll. Their close living is not the Mexican version of *The Brady Bunch*. They are forced to dwell with relatives and strangers whose behavior they would not tolerate except for the interdependent poverty of their circumstances. I don't speak of this in-between world with great authority. I am uncomfortable when people praise me for the "good that I am doing in Santa Ana." I don't know that I do much good at all. In order to persuade our funders and donors to assist us in our work, I talk about the significant number of young people who access Taller San Jose's programs. And it is true. Every year we work with about 500 young people who are in very bad circumstances. But in the end, we just walk with one person at a time. Acculturation is neither a natural nor a linear process and the journey from poverty to economic self-reliance is a long and difficult path. Sometimes we stop with them along the way. They're afraid to go forward for fear of not being able to find the route back if things don't work out on the other side—in the American way.

I founded Taller San Jose in 1995 so that young people who were lost, stuck, or beaten down by life would have someplace to go when they were tired of their troubles. *Taller* is a Spanish word. It means workshop. *San Jose* is Spanish for St. Joseph, the patron of workers. I wanted Taller San Jose, this center for youth, to be a place where broken young people could work on their lives. Although the youth who come through the doors often talk as if they are without hope, I don't really believe that this is so. Here is where my optimism enters. I believe that every one of us carries a small spark of hope within us and that no matter how low its glow, it can be fanned into flame by love.

My love is impatient. I want to see these young people emerge from gangs and drugs and poverty. I want to know if we are making a difference in their lives. What I am allowed to see is some success, some failure, some tentative steps forward, some disappointing stalls, one uncertain step at a time—forward, sideways, backward, onward—the gawky dance of the late adolescent maneuvering between two cultures.

I live by faith, which means I live with uncertainty—not seeing clearly and yet believing. I am not certain of anything. Yet I believe that God has called me to walk between these two worlds and I believe that the God who created us all cares for us equally and that He has given us to each other to care for in His name. I believe that God looks upon each of his creatures as precious—*precioso*—no matter what our sins, no matter how circuitous our earthly paths.

I am allowed to walk between these two worlds because I have the right credentials. I don't have a master's degree in social work, nor am I perfectly fluent in Spanish. Rather, my credentials are the proof of commonality—the self-understanding that I, too, am wounded and in need, that I am sometimes angry and afraid. It is the realization that my worldly goods are no measure of my wealth; in matters of the spirit I too am poor. Like many human beings, I wear a badge of low self-esteem, though I keep mine under wraps. I prefer the cover of competence and success.

It is because of our common humanity that these young people let me walk alongside them. It is because I have been dissed and have dissed others that I know the pain of rejection. If I understand in some small way the intensity of their hatreds and their fears, it is because I have hated and been afraid. Because I am sometimes vulnerable and alone, I can understand the comforting seduction of a gang who claims you as their own and who promises the unconditional love that only God can give.

My story, the life-journey of an American Catholic nun, and the journeys of my young Mexican American friends are intertwined. It is what we share in common that gives me entry into their lives.

Eileen McNerney, CSJ

INTRODUCTION TO TERMS

barrio—a Mexican American neighborhood

beaner—a derogatory term for a Mexican or Mexican American

dissed—to have been disrespected, not treated properly

gabacho(a)—a white man or woman, whitey

ganas—will or drive combined with persistence

homeboys, homies—male Hispanic gang members

jump-in—the ritual of beating a new recruit in order to initiate him to gang life

jump-out—where two or more gang members fight a fellow gang member in order for him to quit the gang

maleducado—poorly educated, especially having poor manners

maquiladora—a foreign-owned factory on the Mexican side of the border

morenita—a dark-skinned Mexican woman, an affectionate name for Our Lady of Guadalupe

motherhouse—the headquarters or central house of a congregation of Catholic nuns

el norte—north of the border, the United States

pocho—A Mexican born in America. It is not an all out insult, but neither is it a term of endearment. Whether it is an insult is determined by who says it and how it is said

precioso—precious

primo(a)—cousin

puta—a whore, prostitute

quinciñiera—a celebration common in Mexico and the Southwest to celebrate the coming-of-age of fifteen-year-old young women

taller—a workshop: (1) a place to build or repair (2) a seminar or training session

Taller San Jose—St. Joseph's Workshop, an education and job-training program for Hispanic young adults in Santa Ana, California

tilma—the cloak worn by Juan Diego, in which he gathered roses as instructed by the Virgin of Guadalupe

Trappistines—a common term for Cistercian nuns, a Catholic religious order of women who live a contemplative and penitential lifestyle

veterano—a long-term gang member, most often someone who has spent time in prison

CHAPTER ONE

I remember when life changed forever and everything stopped getting better.

—J. David Lopez

Javier Ponce and Armando Ibarra were the last two people I expected to see at our convent doorstep. It was dark out. When I turned on the porch light, I could see that they were nervous, their bodies taut and jumpy. Armando didn't say anything, but Javier's expressive eyes caught mine. This was no social visit; somebody was in trouble.

"How did you find my house?" I asked.

"We kept driving around until we saw your car," Javier answered. "We were here before. We remembered the street."

I ushered them into our living room, the least-used room in our house. They sat down on the edge of the sofa and I pulled up a chair.

Armando was a wiry, scrawny kid. At nineteen, he had the stature and the undefined body of a preadolescent. His face was older though—serious, and his eyes were wary. Javier was a stocky and muscular eighteen-year-old. His head sat like an eager pumpkin atop his broad neck. Both of the boys had closely clipped haircuts that signaled their allegiance to a gang.

"Tell her," Javier said and motioned to Armando.

"Javier made me come." It was all Armando could muster.

We sat in silence knowing that there was some truth to be told.

"*¿Que pasa,* Armando?" I asked. "Are you in trouble?"

"Can we go someplace private?" he asked in a muted voice.

What could be more private than the quiet living room of a convent, I thought. I saw that he was glancing through the doorway. The other nuns were cleaning up in the kitchen. He thought they could hear him.

I got up and closed the door.

"Tell her," Javier said again. He wasn't going to say Armando's words for him.

"This girl says I raped her," Armando blurted out. He wasn't looking at me when he said it, but then he glanced up to read my reaction. "The police are looking for me," he continued, "I can't go home."

The sofa on which they were sitting made into a bed, the one we used for guests. I couldn't picture Armando spending the night in the convent.

"Did you rape her?" I asked, praying that he hadn't.

"No."

His monosyllabic response didn't tell me anything.

"Did you have sex with her?" I asked.

"Yeh."

"Where were you?"

"In my car."

"Who is she?" I sounded like an interrogator.

"I don't know her name," he admitted. "I met her at a party. We were both drinking."

"How old is she?" I asked. I wanted all the relevant information up front. I wondered if the girl was a minor.

"I think she's over eighteen," Javier popped in.

"Tell me what happened, Armando," I plied. "Why is she saying that you raped her?"

"She told her sister that I raped her and her sister called the police. But I didn't. She said she wanted to do it. She took off her clothes. The police already came to my house. My mother told them I didn't live there anymore. I can't go home."

I wasn't feeling proud of Armando and I was confused and angry. I didn't feel certain that he was telling me the whole story and I didn't like to think of him or any of our guys having anonymous sex with nameless girls. Rape or not, he used this girl, paying no attention to the consequences. I claimed Armando as one of our Taller San Jose boys. He'd been around awhile, struggling with drugs and clinging to the edge of a gang, but Taller San Jose was his home base. He kept coming back, depositing his hope with us as if we were a bank and trusting us to safeguard his future. If the police had a warrant out for his arrest, they were going to find him.

"What do you want to do?" I asked.

"I could go to Mexico," he responded.

"I hate to see you run, Armando," I cautioned. "You'll be running and hiding your whole life. If you say you didn't do it, and you think you can prove it, stand up for yourself."

"I didn't rape her," he said, louder and stronger this time.

"He can stay with me tonight," Javier offered, "but my mom won't let him stay for a long time."

"If you want to keep working at Taller," I said, "you'll have to deal with the police. But we can help you. I want you to talk with Art Guerrero tomorrow.

Art was our point man on staff for dealing with criminal behavior. He was a former federal probation officer and he kept a cool head.

"Are you willing to do that? Will you come tomorrow and meet with Art?"

Armando nodded his assent. I wasn't sure how strong it was. He was scared.

I said a quiet prayer with them, asking God to give Armando the strength to stand up to his fears.

The kitchen was quiet now. The other nuns were in the chapel when I walked the boys to the door.

"Thanks for being a nun and stuff," Javier offered. "We need you."

I gave each of the boys a hug. Armando hugged me stiffly. But he had always been a stiff hugger. He wasn't that comfortable with himself.

"I'll see you tomorrow," I ventured.

"Yeh, okay," he muttered, "tomorrow."

Armando did meet with Art Guerrero, a Taller San Jose counselor, who accompanied him to the police station the next day to face any charges made against him. Ultimately his name was cleared, but that didn't mean he'd matured, deepened his value system, or learned to take responsibility for his actions. Both Armando and Javier spent over two years at Taller San Jose, wrestling with their drug issues, easing the hold that the gang had on them, and growing from boys to men.

When I first became a nun, I couldn't have imagined working with Javier Ponce and Armando Ibarra. In my youth, I just wanted to be a good person, to be of service, to have God make good use of my life providing that I could avoid risk, inconvenience, and suffering. It took me a long time to find the place where my deep gladness and the world's deep hunger meet—on the streets of Santa Ana. By the time I found this place, my safety and security were no longer of concern to me. I had had a good life, filled with opportunity and privilege, but I could see that many of the young people on the streets of Santa Ana were dying. Either they were killing each other, drugging their souls into a lifeless stupor, or giving up on life before they'd even lived it. I remembered a phrase I'd seen in a medical textbook describing infants who had been born healthy but who were "failing to thrive." What the babies needed was love, the sense that someone cared about them very deeply, that someone was investing in them. I began to understand that these young people in Santa Ana—those who were giving up on life too soon needed the same.

CHAPTER TWO

*People try to tell me what to think or say, but my thoughts
are made from what my eyes have seen.*

—Juan Carrasco

I don't know why I just don't walk to work. God knows I've
thought about it often enough. It's not even a two mile drive from
the home that I share with three other nuns to the bustling corner
of Santa Ana where I pour out what's left to give of my heart. The
drive can be a treacherous one and I am extra cautious when I cross
17th Street. South of 17th Street, pedestrians, mostly women and
children, outnumber the cars in the early morning hours. Some say
that there's no difference from one side of this street to the other.
But that's not true. In Santa Ana, it's 17th Street, not the railroad
tracks, that separates the rich from the poor.

North of 17th Street, the homes range from comfortable to
grand. Many were built in the 1920s, when the economy was
flush and distinctive architectural details were important.
Decades-old trees line these streets—oak, pine, sycamore, and
liquid ambers. Ferny jacarandas display their great lavender bou-
quets each May. The branches of the great trees sometimes
stretch out into the middle of the wide, quiet streets. When they
touch, the boughs form dense green umbrellas, permitting only
narrow shafts of light to penetrate to the street below. The neighborhoods north of 17th Street are soothing, the gardens lush and
cultivated. Giant crows, common sparrows, and a flurry of hum-
mingbirds delight in this verdant forest. From spring through fall,
flocks of raucous green parrots move from one tree to the next,
making their home in the lush foliage. They fly south when
there's a hint that California's mild winter is just days away. And

when it's dark in these soft and comfortable streets and when no one is watching, the possums who've slept away the day edge their way along the fence tops and creep from tree to tree.

South of 17th Street, the neighborhoods are not so pleasant. Midsize to large apartment buildings dominate the single family dwellings on the crowded streets. It's not unusual to find that all the residents of one apartment building come from the same region of Mexico—Zacatecas, Nayarit, Jalisco, or Michoacan. *"Somos de Zamora,"* a resident might proclaim proudly, announcing that all of the inhabitants on the corner come from the same home town. While some apartment owners maintain their rental properties, others are little better than slumlords. The façades of the apartments can be deceptive; it's "the innards"—the stairways, the elevators, and the units themselves that bear the telltale signs of poverty—the grime, the graffiti, and the wear and tear of too many tenants with too many belongings crammed into too tight spaces. In these overcrowded neighborhoods, street vendors vie for space with the older-model used cars that perpetually line the streets. The vendors' trucks are filled with Mexican staples—rice, beans, tortillas, and chiles, but also fresh tomatoes, radishes, cucumbers, tomatillos, avocados, nopales, melons, and mangos.

South of 17th Street, Santa Ana is chiefly a pedestrian city. That's why I drive so very carefully there. On school day mornings, the mothers walk in long processions escorting their children from the safety of one corner to the next—prodding the sleepyheads onward and keeping their more impish offspring from darting in and about the cars and vendors that line the narrow streets. You can hardly see the mothers for the children that surround them and the toddlers and babies that they have in tow.

There's an unspoken directive that governs the interaction between one side of 17th Street and the other. *You stay on your side of the street and everything will be just fine,* the Anglo neighborhoods silently proclaim to the more numerous brown-skinned residents of the city. And with few exceptions—a few Mexican apartment buildings having found their way into the northern neighborhoods—that's the tacit agreement. It's only at Halloween and for quarterly garage sales that the Mexican population crosses to the other side of the divide—to see what the rich are handing out or casting off.

It's 4th Street, *Calle Cuatro,* deeper into Mexican Santa Ana, where one feels the throbbing beat of the city—the buying, selling, and trading in the shops and on the street corners. It is best to speak Spanish here. On 4th Street, the food carts are filled with Mexican delicacies—fresh fruit cocktails, corn on the cob, churros, cucumbers peppered with chili. The ice cream flavors are a taste of Mexico—mango, pineapple, tamarind, guava, coconut, and chili pepper. *Chicharrones,* deep fried slices of pork rind, hang from the sides of the carts like aged and greasy elephant ears.

Eighty percent of Santa Ana's 350,000 residents are of Hispanic origin and over half of the people who now call this city home were born outside the United States. The majority of residents over the age of eighteen have not graduated from high school. And the city is teeming with youth. The average age of Santa Ana residents is 26.7 years. Statistically it has the youngest median age of any city in the country.

Uncounted are numerous Mexican nationals—the undocumented who hide in back bedrooms, crowded apartments, and garages. These undercover residents of the city will take any job for the chance to cling to the edges of life in California. It's the undocumented who bus the tables in the hotels and restaurants, clean the houses, wash the cars, and mow the lawns of the well-to-do. It is they who dig the ditches and do piecework and assembly in the factories by night. It's the way the county works. This undercover trade-off between the rich and the poor has always been so, and although there is grumbling and occasional outrage about the politically incorrect and unjust practices of labor, there are no serious efforts to change the system. One generation after the next, hungry Mexicans find their way across the border in spite of all the fences built to keep them out.

The undocumented residents are fairly hidden from view and happy to remain that way. But the hospitals know that they are there and so do the schools and the police. Without medical insurance, those without proper papers or insurance use the hospital emergency rooms when they are in a medical crisis. The hospitals cannot turn them away. Every school in the city is impacted by the burgeoning population of youngsters. School yards, the broad green fields of the past, have disappeared altogether. Now multiple rows of portable classrooms have reduced the playgrounds to small slabs of concrete.

The police know where the trouble spots are, where the gangs hang out. One gang or another lays claim to each of the Hispanic neighborhoods in Santa Ana, and some areas are more dangerous than others. You can't always tell by looking.

I've come to know this city well. I've lived south of 17th Street and I've lived to the north. It's like two different cities—of that I'm certain.

CHAPTER THREE

*Adrift, floating in the starless night sky, I don't know if I'm
waiting for death or waiting to become alive.*
—Ernie Serrano

I moved to Santa Ana a decade ago. It was in the middle of
my life—or so I thought—and I had developed an uncomfortable
and soulful itch that came from a place deep down within me
where I couldn't get at it to scratch. I didn't have a name for this
mild madness that visited itself upon me, but I came to know its
contours well. I knew how it played out in my mind and heart,
monkeying with me, causing me to feel useless, and filling me
with doubt about the meaning and purpose of my life. I knew that
if I didn't pay attention to my distress that within a few months,
maybe sooner, I would likely enter a period of depression.

Winston Churchill gave his depression a name, "the black
dog." He described in dark images the dog's heavy weight
enveloping his body, mind, and spirit. Churchill cursed the dog's
own unwillingness to move and his own incapacity to lift the
dreaded canine off of him.

It's embarrassing for a Catholic nun to admit to melancholy
while following the Lord Jesus Christ. The awkward contradic-
tion of it could be described in the lyrics of a country western,
How Can I Feel So Bad When I'm Doin' So Right? When my soul
is afflicted, I feel shame. I often keep the darkness to myself.

Alone, I was stuck in a vertical tunnel—a sort of people-
sized tin can. The smooth curved sides defined the boundaries of
my life, but where my feet were supposed to touch down, there
was no floor. With no grab bars to hold on to and no ground
under my feet, I flailed about in midair. There was no hint of the

path ahead. I hadn't known that nuns got lost along the way. If they did, no one talked about it.

I have an image of the "good nun." She is prayerful, plucky, and has a constancy that is renewed each morning. I live under the illusion that most nuns are "good nuns" and that I am a bit of a faith-filled aberration. When I am depressed I avoid prayer, for authentic prayer requires that one look reality in the face. When my soul is spent and I am without a passion for life, I lie in bed in the morning until I feel guilty enough to get up. Meanwhile, I let the "good nuns" carry on without me.

I've learned to view depression as a dark friend who carries an important message. The longer I leave the friend waiting on the doorstep, the more paralyzed and fearful I become. But if I invite the unwelcome guest in for a cup of tea, I will learn what is weighing on my mind and heart. When I face my fears, I'm able to get on with my life, even if my verve doesn't kick in right from the start.

Reluctantly I embraced the solitude of my midlife journey. Inwardly, I pushed at the edges that defined my life. I questioned whether I was living my religious vows to the full. The vows of poverty, chastity, and obedience are not meant to set nuns above others in holiness but are rather meant to free one to live the gospel in a radical and direct way. I wondered if I had compromised my vows that I had taken in my youth, selling out to the comforts and enticements of the world around me. The issue for me, whether or not I could define it, was that my life had become too safe. I had a sense that I needed to break through this level of comfort in order to live the rest of my life more wholly, but I didn't know what it was that I had to break through or how I was to do it. And so I set myself to waiting for answers and I prayed to wait without anxiety.

It was during this time that I started to attend Sunday Mass each week in Spanish. I didn't invite anyone to go with me and I rarely spoke of my experience. At the Spanish Mass, I was one more dark-haired worshipper in the crowd, though I was a head taller than all of the women and some of the men in the church. I was also a stranger. I didn't know anyone and no one acknowledged me. My Spanish was poor, even though my father had insisted that my sister and I study it for years when we were young.

"Don't forget you're Mexican," was his way of reminding us of the thin Hispanic bloodline passed on to us by our forebears, a number of whom had come to California from Baja California and Sonora in the latter part of the eighteenth century.

The churches in the Mexican barrios were always full of people. When the people overflowed the church buildings, they circled the church, clinging to it, as if touching the building counted for something. There were multitudes of squirming babies in the church, and toddlers ran about seemingly unattended but within the watchful eye of a parent who was ready to scoop them up at the first sign of trouble. Sometimes there was a wondrous group of homespun musicians; at other times a few brave souls formed a makeshift choir and belted out dissonant melodies like a herd of gray, stray Mexican alley cats. Many people in the church knew all the verses to all of the songs by heart as if the words were emblazoned like DNA on the Mexican soul.

I looked forward to this sanctuary on Sunday mornings. My restless heart felt at home here. During the quiet time of the Mass I reflected about why I was drawn to this experience and an unconscious call began to take form within me. I knew that some day I would be working with people from Mexico.

That's when I stopped driving the freeways and started to explore the Mexico that had grown around me. For as far back as anyone could remember, there have been Mexican barrio neighborhoods in Orange County. Mexicans had always lived where there were oranges to be picked and packed and where the sugar beets were harvested and processed. The barrios today stand where the groves and the fields once reigned—Logan and Delhi in Santa Ana, El Modena in Orange. One generation after the next, people had come up from Mexico to California. There were jobs in California and money to be sent back home. And then in the 1980s, the Hispanic population in Orange County exploded.

Now for the first time I saw neighborhoods where thousands of people occupied a few square blocks of run-down apartments. Sometimes I would pull the car over and watch the bustle of an unfamiliar neighborhood. Tough-looking kids hung about the corners and sat on the curbs. Bare-chested beer drinkers with elaborate tattoos leaned against parked cars. Young moms with baby carriages milled about, toddlers clinging to their legs. It was a strong contrast to my neighborhood, where our convent was nestled among homes valued at a half-million dollars and where self-sufficient neighbors politely nodded to each other from their cars as they entered and exited their garages each day. Where I lived, neighbors didn't need each other. We barely knew each others' names.

One weekday morning, I drove east on Chapman Avenue toward the hills of Orange. I hadn't taken this route in the early hours before and I was astonished by the number of Mexican immigrant day laborers who gathered on the street corners. Brown-skinned men huddled in groups of six or eight to a corner on both sides of the street for well over a mile. This spelled trouble in the city of Orange. This was a conservative community and not yet ready to see itself as a haven for immigrants. Chapman Avenue was a wide, pretty street with well-kept and landscaped properties. Behind the polished storefronts though, on either side of the street, was a very old barrio, El Modena. Mexican people had lived in El Modena for generations—many in small, substandard bungalows. Originally the residents had been agricultural workers; now they took any bottom level job available in the county. Recent immigration had swelled the population of the El Modena barrio and the men on the street corners were evidence of this. A week later, I read in the paper about INS raids in El Modena.

The raids were targeted toward the Villa Santiago Apartments. I drove out to see the place—sixty aging two story apartment buildings, leaning on each other for survival. Everything about the place was cheap and slumlike. There were no garages or parking structures. Junker cars overlapped the streets onto walkways. The whole place was a dump—and well hidden from the main thoroughfare. There was a single point of entry and exit to the complex. Giant wrought iron fences blocked off all other points of access. If the INS chose to raid this area, the residents were trapped in a giant holding pen. Who had blocked off the streets? Did the occupants know that they didn't have to live this way? What on earth did they pay for the privilege of living there?

My new consciousness about poverty and immigration in Orange County began to change me. With hindsight, I was doing what I was trained to do from the moment I entered the convent—paying attention to the neighbor, especially people who were in the greatest need. When the Sisters of St. Joseph first emerged in France in 1650, it was a troubled time. There was a huge economic gap between the rich and the poor. While a few enjoyed the comfort and the privileges of wealth, the masses were hurting. Jean Pierre Medaille, a Jesuit priest, gathered together women who cared about the problems of their day. He helped the women to deepen their spiritual lives and at the same time taught them how to organize and how to address the needs in their own neighborhoods. He gave the first nuns a basic instruction that all Sisters of St. Joseph throughout the world still carry in their hearts. Translated from seventeenth-century French, the words sound formal to our modern ears, but the content remains relevant. *"Divide the city in quarters and go out into the neighborhoods to determine what kind of ills you find and when you have found needs that are not being met, find worthy people to help you to meet them."*

I was discovering in concrete detail that not unlike seventeenth-century France, Orange County had a huge economic gap between the rich and the poor. I observed that while many enjoyed the comfort and the privileges of wealth, others lived in poverty and want. I saw myself as one who lived in great comfort.

It was 1990. I was fifty years old. I didn't know what to do about what I was seeing and so for the moment, I just stood still and watched.

CHAPTER FOUR

We have been doing this for so many years and what has it gotten us? More prison terms and more Chicanos being sent to their graves at an early age. More heads getting bashed against walls, more innocent people and children getting hit by stray bullets. If we must shed our blood on this earth, let it be for the good and protection of our people and not for our own self-destruction.

—Angelica Morales

My path out of darkness came in the oddest way—through reading the obituaries. The obituaries were in the local section of the paper, the section that covers the news of fatal traffic accidents and nearby homicides, so that's when I started to read the frequent news clips about young men shot and killed on the streets in Santa Ana. "Seventeen-Year-old Youth Killed in Drive-by Shooting," "Gang Drive-By Kills 1, Injures 3," "Gang-Related Bullet Misses Mark, Kills Toddler."

Who were these kids who were killing each other? I wondered. *What is going on inside of them that allows them to maim and to kill? Aren't they afraid for their own lives?* There were seventy-one homicides in Santa Ana in 1991. I was horrified, but I wasn't certain what these atrocities had to do with me. The world of the young, Hispanic gang members seemed very far from my own.

My wanderings amidst the immigrant communities awakened in me a desire to learn Spanish. I asked for a month free from my work to attend a language school in Mexico and I found a group of nuns in the city of Morelia, Michoacan, who agreed to let me live with them. The Mexican nuns included me in all their activities. Their conversation was often warm and familial and far beyond my range of comprehension. In spite of my best efforts, I was often mute. I wanted to let the nuns know how smart, funny, deep, compassionate, and clever I was, but I was none of these things in Spanish. It didn't matter. The Mexican nuns surrounded me with the grace of their quiet acceptance.

Learning a new language is tedious and sometimes I cried in frustration. But I applied myself mightily to my studies and, over time, my Spanish did improve. Before my stay in Mexico, I had only been able to communicate in simple phrases and I rarely understood what was spoken to me. In Mexico, my listening skills improved. I began to decode what was being said to me and when I didn't understand everything, I was able to fill in the blanks. One syllable, one word at a time, I became a better Spanish speaker.

When I returned from Mexico, one of the nuns with whom I was living asked me if I'd be interested in teaching English to day laborers at the hiring hall in Orange. I said, "Sure." I was looking for some way to insert myself into the Spanish-speaking world, and the class time fit in with my schedule. The class was offered at 6:30 a.m. on Tuesday mornings.

The hiring hall was a central gathering point for day laborers who were seeking work. The City of Orange financed it in an effort to keep the men off the street. The hiring hall sponsored English classes for the workers while they waited for employers to drive by with offers of day work. Carmen Saldaña, a gritty Hispanic woman in her early forties, managed the operation, which meant dealing with both workers and employers—99 percent of whom were men. Nobody messed with Carmen. She governed three large, clear fish bowls that fronted her desk and the fish bowls were key to the whole enterprise. Each man who wanted to work had to register and was assigned a code number. If he spoke limited English, he put his number in bowl #1; if he spoke no English, bowl #2; if he had transportation and could get himself to the work site and home, bowl #3. Cars and pick-up trucks drove up throughout the morning looking for men to do roofing, gardening, painting, and clean-up work. The pay was minimal and unregulated—whatever the employer wanted to offer, whatever the worker would accept. Sometimes the employer would drive the men for miles to a job site and then they would have to find their own way home. The men who could speak a little English and had a car had the best chance to find a job. Day after day the same routine prevailed. When I drove up each Tuesday morning, the guys would be rolling over the fence that separated their apartments from the hiring hall. On the other side of the fence were the grim Villa Santiago Apartments.

The small classroom inside the hiring hall was spare and square. A circular table with ten chairs filled the room. A white board and some markers were the only supplies. My students, all men, ranged in age from seventeen to fifty and they came from every part of Mexico but chiefly from the area around Veracruz. The young ones were sent up here, *el norte*, to help support their families back home. The older ones had been coming back and forth across the border for years, hoping to save enough money to build a small home in Mexico—a goal that was often elusive. They were willing and eager students. Our lessons focused on basic words and phrases that would help them to get through their day with some sense of dignity and keep them from being cheated or abused by the employer. From time to time during the class, Carmen Saldaña would knock at the door and call out a number. And then one of the students would beam with delight, jump up, and bolt out the door. A day's work was a big prize. Every day nearly two hundred men waited for work; maybe sixty were selected.

Some of the men gathered long before dawn, hoping to improve their opportunity for employment. The fewer numbers that were in the glass bowls when the employers came to choose lots, the better chance they had of getting work for the day. It reminded me of the story in the gospel where some laborers in the vineyard worked all day and others worked for far less time, but all received the same pay. But this wasn't just about working but also waiting, waiting all day and finding no work, or waiting just a little and happily being among the chosen. It was all meant to be fair, this luck of the draw. But when I looked in the faces of the men and saw their hopelessness or when I grasped their hands and was enveloped by the beefy, callused muscles of hard labor, I was reminded that life wasn't fair at all. By the luck of the draw, my great-grandparents from south of the border had traveled north to California with the Franciscan friars and their military entourage in the eighteenth century. Two hundred years later, I was born white and privileged. These poor day laborers and their ancestors had been born and bred in the pueblos of rural Mexico and now these men were standing beside me scrounging for survival in the land of plenty.

From the men I learned the gross indignity of working without skills or education and without any safety precautions whatsoever. I saw how years of hard labor had beaten down the bodies of men who were not even forty years old. I saw men climb into trucks delighted to have work for the day—yet not knowing what kind of work they would be doing, how they would be treated, or how much they would be paid. That kind of work, repeated day after day, beat down not only their bodies but also their spirits. In the three years that I spent teaching the men and conversing with them, I learned that these men were not inclined to be in trouble with the law. The day laborers, even the young ones, were not gang members. They were day-to-day survivors just trying to earn enough money to pay the rent and eat so that they could send money back to their families in Mexico. They might drink too much and get into fights, but their souls were on the other side of the border—they weren't looking for trouble.

Every Tuesday morning when I arrived at the hiring hall, the men were out in front, leaning against the porch or clumped around the few benches clasping Styrofoam cups of steaming coffee to warm their hands. Carmen recruited my first students but it didn't seem right to continue to lean on her for this; so every Tuesday morning I moved from circle to circle describing the class as best I could and inviting the men in—if only to get warm! I was dressed for my workday, looking serious and polished. They had on yesterday's work clothes. Some of the men just stared at me—Mexican men can do that. I pushed onward, offering the opportunity for learning to the old-timers and newcomers, young and old. I always had a lot of takers.

We practiced the same phrases over and over again. Survival words. I wanted them to know what kind of work they might be doing that day and how much they would be making and if they would get a ride back home or be set adrift twenty miles away at the end of the day's work. I wanted them to know these things before they hopped into a truck with a fatalistic attitude. Did they want this dignity as badly as I wanted them to have it? I guess some of them did, because they looked for me every Tuesday morning and they found their way into the bleak, little classroom.

"Do you want to work?" I exaggerated each word, consonant, and syllable.

English is spoken more crisply than Spanish, harder consonants, crisper endings.

"Miren los labios," I said, pointing to my lips.

"Do you want to work?" Those were the real words, the correct pronunciation and grammar, but the words didn't sound like that when a construction boss drove by, rolled down his window, and gestured to the waiting men from the side of the road.

"Hey, ya wanna work?" I did my best imitation of their imaginary boss-for-the-day in a husky, masculine John Wayne-like swagger.

I remembered the tears that I'd shed in Mexico sweating over my Spanish studies, and so I tried to make them laugh. You take more risks in a new language when you can laugh.

Over time, I learned to hear and understand their Spanish—Spanish spoken in rural Mexico, sometimes bad Spanish, poorly enunciated Spanish. I learned words that weren't in the dictionary. Bad words. This is what I needed to learn if my rudimentary Spanish skills were going to be of any use to me. In the end, there were two forms of Spanish that I couldn't understand at all—Spanish spoken through a pungent, musty blur of alcohol and the Spanish muttered by the men who had lost all their teeth.

I was beginning to learn some things about the growing Hispanic population in Orange County, but from where I lived in northeast Fullerton and how I spent my days behind a desk, I might as well have been a thousand miles away. I began to think about moving. I drove by the rental office of the Villa Santiago Apartments, across the fence from the hiring hall, and took down the phone number of the manager. I was too timid to go in. I called to inquire about the cost of an apartment—$900 a month for two tiny bedrooms and one bath, no garage! I had already seen the condition of the apartments. The high cost of rent was simply inconceivable to me. No wonder the men that I taught lived six or more to an apartment crowded against each other with bedrolls on the floor.

I made an appointment to see the pastor in the nearby parish. I introduced myself. I asked him what he knew about the situation in these apartments and what he knew about the people in his parish who lived in the Villa Santiago Apartments. I confided to him my desire to ask some Sisters of St. Joseph to move with me into one of the miserable apartments. I asked his advice. I hadn't met the pastor before, but I'd seen him. He was fairly young, blond, good-looking, and distant. I tried not to sound overly eager or naïve. He listened while I poured out my heart.

When I was finished, the handsome blond responded, "You'll have to talk with Father Gabriel. He deals with the Mexicans." End of conversation.

I recalled a reading from the liturgy that morning,

For the Lord is the judge, and with him there is no partiality. He will not show partiality to the poor; but he will listen to the prayer of one who is wronged (Sir 35:15–16).

Really? I wondered. *How will the wronged know when they are heard?*

CHAPTER FIVE

*Gang life?…it's a big circle going round and round, killing
each other slowly but surely. Maybe we should all go out in
the middle of the street and have a big shoot-out so we can
kill one another at the same time.*

—Angelica Morales

I've got to move…got to move soon, my heart insisted each
morning when I awakened.

Years before, I had memorized only one passage from the
documents of the Second Vatican Council. It was the opening
line from *Gaudium et Spes: The joys and hopes, the griefs and the
anxieties of the people of this age, especially those who are poor or in
any way afflicted, these too are the joys and hopes, the griefs and anxieties of the followers of Christ.*

I was a follower of Christ—a Catholic nun—and I had been
reading about the griefs and anxieties of the poor from the comfort of my living room. I became convinced that this disparity
between my convictions and my reality was the touchstone of my
restlessness. If I was to make a move, I first had to talk with my
general superior, Sister Nancy O'Connor. I wasn't an independent agent; I followed marching orders. Her approval was key to
my plan. When I told her about my wanderings in the neighborhoods, about my experience with the day laborers, about my on-
going prayer, and my conviction that the Sisters of St. Joseph
ought to be present in the Villa Santiago Apartment complex, she
agreed to visit the place with me.

The next day we drove to the site of the run-down apartments. I had grown used to the misery of the place. I'd prayed
about this move. But for Nancy, it was a first visit. She was very

quiet in the car as I drove her up and down the grim streets. It was a gray, February day and the Villa Santiago Apartments looked more dreadful than usual. Screens were torn and falling off the windows. Duct tape covered cracks and breakages. Men, clasping cans of beer, leaned against a multitude of broken and beat-up cars.

We stopped for lunch on the way home. Nancy's ruminating silence told me that she didn't like the place. She was a worrier and she was the top boss, after all. Fretting went with the job. Nancy boldly tended the mission of the Sisters of St. Joseph, but she was also vigilant about looking after the safety and well-being of the sisters. She suggested that I look for a house instead of an apartment and she indicated her preference for the neighborhood around St. Joseph's Church in Santa Ana.

Damn it, I thought but didn't say, *I don't want you watching over me. I don't want you protecting me. I'm ready to move to Villa Santiago tomorrow. I don't want to go through a year-long search that will get hopelessly buried in convent red tape.*

When we got back to the Motherhouse, I went into the chapel to process my disappointment. I felt fussed and edgy and so I sat in silence trying to calm my soul. It took me several minutes before I realized that Nancy had squelched the move to the Villa Santiago area, but not the move itself. Nancy had said, "Yes!" I just needed to find a house and I needed to find one in the city of Santa Ana.

I concentrated my search for a house on the French Park and Lacy neighborhoods close to St. Joseph's Church in the center of town. Every day when I had a bit of free time, I drove up and down the streets of Santa Ana looking for my new home.

I found the house one day on the corner of 5th Street and Minter Avenue. The neighborhood had seen better days. A homemade sign in the window caught my eye as I drove by—"4 sale; 4 bedrooms; 2 baths." The old gray house was empty and weary but in its prime, a hundred years before, it might have belonged to anyone's grandmother. A wide wrap-around porch skirted the front and side and it had a big, fenced yard in the back. The streets were lined with a crazy mix of aging rental homes and large apartment buildings with a bit of quirky light industry thrown in. There was a grim tire repair shop across the street and ice cream trucks were stored in a nearby yard. A year's trash had collected in an empty lot and papered the cyclone fence that enclosed the property.

I went to the house next door to ask if the neighbors knew anything about the corner house for sale. A tall, gawky kid, who hadn't yet grown into the size of his head, stared at me from behind the locked screen door and offered me an unintelligible, monosyllabic grunt. I felt really stupid. I was a *gabacha*, I guess, a white woman in the wrong neighborhood. Without a word, he turned and left me standing there alone, but when he returned he brought his grandfather with him. The toothless old man muttered in Spanish and I barely understood him. He told me that the owner wanted $190,000 for the property. I didn't think the Sisters of St. Joseph wanted to pay that much for a broken down old house and I hoped that I could talk the owner into a lease.

As I turned to walk back to my car, five sullen young men skirted past me on the narrow sidewalk. Their demeanor was meant to threaten. The muscles in my throat tightened. A strong, dark spirit surrounded them and threatened to pull me into its perimeter. So young they were, and yet their eyes were shut down, signaling that something essential had died deep down within them. It was my first chilling encounter with the gang.

The little, gray house on the corner of 5th Street and Minter Avenue was to become my home for the next five years. The house had a lot of problems that had to be addressed before we could move in. The landlord had previously divided the interior so that he could rent it to two families, but neither side of the house was complete. There was no functioning kitchen and the gas hadn't been connected properly and so some of the residents had cooked on a portable barbecue perched on the rickety back porch. Indeed, there were two bathrooms but one was a small half-bath and the other made the words "water closet" seem elegant. The back porch and fence were rotting and had to be replaced. It had been a stately little house in its day with lovely old crown molding and built-in cupboards, but the woodwork had long since been covered over with numerous coats of thick, gloppy paint. There was no central heat—a given that we had to live with. Still, the old house had character.

One Saturday I asked Kathleen and Jayne, two of the nuns that I lived with if they would drive down to Santa Ana with me to check out the noise level in the neighborhood at night. And so on the next weekend we piled in the car and sat in front of the house between 8:30 and 9:00 p.m. There were a few cars passing by, a bit of foot traffic but nothing very disturbing.

And so four of us moved in—Rebecca, Jeanne, Louise Ann, and I—during the first week of August 1992. The moving van arrived from the Motherhouse with a lot of second-hand furniture and household items from storage. The big van drew a lot of attention from the neighbors. I wanted the movers to unload our items quickly and get on their way. None of our new neighbors had the money to hire a moving van or the possessions to require one. Throughout the day, people from the nearby apartments kept coming out to stare at our furniture and at us.

I inherited the tiny bedroom at the back of the house. The ceiling was very low and there was no closet. The room was an add-on to the house, an afterthought—more of a box than a room. This pocketsize space was poorly insulated for both weather and noise so that when I lay in bed at night, I had the illusion that my head was in the street. One night as I was drifting off to sleep, gunshots rang out at such a close range that I imagined I could have been the intended victim. The smell of gunpowder filled my nostrils. I sat bolt upright in bed. A second later I rolled onto the floor. I lay there as still as possible, my heart pounding and my body pressed to the carpet. I thought about all the incidents that

I read about when stray bullets from gang fights had shot straight through exterior walls, killing occupants within.

The next day I moved my bed so that less of me was exposed to the outside wall. We heard gunshots every night—sometimes close by, at other times within blocks. Sometimes afterward, there were shouting and sirens; at other times there was just an eerie silence. I slept, but lightly, ever-coasting on the edge of a deeper slumber—subconsciously vigilant. One night I heard rustling outside my little bedroom window. I rolled over, parted the blinds, and peeked out. Some guy was peeing on my rose bush. It was 3:00 a.m.

Our neighbors had a decades-old avocado tree, a giant umbrella of leaves that covered the entire roof of their house. Nearly half of the tree leaned into our yard and provided us with magnificent shade—and plenty of avocados in season. One morning as I was cleaning up after breakfast, I looked out our kitchen window and saw a man sleeping on the neighbor's roof under the shade of the great tree. His perch on the roof was so close to our house that I could see the rise and fall of his chest and hear his rhythmic snore.

From that same window we had a view of the neighbor's garage. The family who lived in the garage, Jorge and Catalina Vasquez and their children, had lived there for fourteen years. It was the only home that the children had ever known. Their living space was very simple—a cement floor, bare light bulbs suspended from the ceiling and a curtain that separated the beds of the three children from that of their parents. There was no heat or plumbing, just a trough outside where they washed up. They used a bathroom that was attached to the main house by a plumbing hook up. It looked more like an outhouse. They were part of an extended family that shared the main house and that is where they cooked and ate.

Except for the Ornelas family, who lived next door, the Vasquez family in the garage and the Payans, who lived behind us, it was hard to meet the neighbors. When new families moved into the neighborhood, we made an effort to introduce ourselves and welcome them. But nobody stayed long. Although the housing was poor, it was also costly. Over time I learned that this wasn't a settled neighborhood at all, but rather a point of entry for many new residents from south of the border. When people didn't have the money to keep up the rent and the wolves were at the door, they moved in the middle of the night under cover of darkness. One day we could be talking to neighbors and the next day they were gone; disappeared with no forwarding information. Most of the time they didn't say goodbye. Many of our neighbors were undocumented—illegal aliens in the eyes of the law. They were careful not to reveal too much—neither to us nor to each other. There were a lot of sleazy people in our neighborhood, too, and a number of regular drug sellers and buyers. It wasn't what I imagined—this poor, dense living. It wasn't a community. In the Lacy neighborhood, desperately poor people lived side by side in transient desperation—until they could move on. Life at 5th Street and Minter Avenue was grim.

Our corner was a drug dealer's paradise. Not only did the locals load up on supplies each day, but drivers from out of town in fancy BMWs and Jaguars turned off 4th Street, the main drag, for quick, drive-by, drug purchases. A sallow looking character claimed the local drug market. No matter how he dressed for the day, he topped off his outfit with a dark blue baseball cap with the word "Navy" printed boldly in white. "Navy" had a lean and hungry look about him like a coyote down on his luck. Sometimes when the sales were going on, we called the police; sometimes they came. We couldn't do it every day; we had to get about our life and stop looking out the window. At times it all seemed futile. The sight of "Navy" sickened me.

One afternoon three little neighbor girls visited us and told us that the man next door had died.

"What man?" we asked in Spanish. "The grandfather?"

"No," the kids replied. "The son. He died in the bathtub."

Sister Rebecca went over to get the story. It was true. Miguel Ornelas had died; he overdosed on heroin in the bathtub. He was forty-three years old. The coroner had just left the house.

Every night, for nine consecutive nights, we went over to the neighbors to say the rosary with them for their son. They had made a kind of shrine to Miguel, their wayward son, and surrounded his picture with statues, candles, and flowers. There was a whole ritual of prayers to be said in Spanish with tamales and other treats to follow. Clearly, Miguel had been the black sheep of the family. They all knew that he was on drugs and they were always worried about him. He hadn't held a job in years. They were sad, but there were no tears. Miguel had a teenage son who was following his father's path. At eighteen, Miguel Jr. was a gang member and also a drug user. Some of the family members hadn't talked with one another in years—who knew what the hurts were—but they all came for Miguel's funeral. The Ornelas family never went to church, but all the praying, the home altar, the rosary, and our presence were very important to them. They were reluctant to let the memory of their errant son and brother fade into darkness. Throughout the nine day grieving ritual, they clung to Miguel's spirit—willing him a better life in the hereafter than the one he'd spent on earth.

St. Joseph's Church was just a block and a half away from our home but not many people from our druggy, transient neighborhood went to church—maybe ten percent. And yet the three Sunday Masses in Spanish there were filled to overflowing with worshippers from the streets that surrounded us. If you were far from your homeland—Mexico, El Salvador, or Guatemala, the familiarity of the liturgy in your native tongue and the music of your childhood was healing and comforting.

I love that church. It is a holy place to me. Early in the morning the soft light of the new day filters in through the high, amber windows. It flows over the sanctuary first and as the sun slowly rises it bathes the rest of the church in a warm glow. Some people say it's too dark in there—because of the wooden beams, I guess. But it's not too dark for me. I can always find God in St. Joseph's Church—or God finds me—whoever is looking harder for the other at the moment.

Father Christopher Smith, the pastor, plays an important role in the neighborhood. He has a commitment to the community and the people know it. It's not like it's a stopping off place for him while he's waiting to advance to a higher rank in Church circles. He's a real pastor, a shepherd. His presence is a symbol of stability and hope among much poverty and chaos.

When gang tensions were at their height, a stray bullet struck and killed a small child in the midst of a gang shoot-out, knocking him from his father's arms. The horror of it outraged the whole of the city. Father Christopher, who has an innate sense of how to help heal inexplicable social pain, led a procession through the streets to ask God's blessing of peace on the neighborhood. He chose Palm Sunday for the day of the solemn march. The parents of the child who had been killed walked right behind Christopher as he held the Blessed Sacrament high so that everyone could see. They were a young couple, still in their twenties, and their two other young children walked next to them, clinging to their hands and clutching their clothing.

From my little room at the back of our house on the corner, I heard gunshots almost every night. When the shots were very close, we huddled under the windows and peeked out. Sister Rebecca was bolder than the rest of us and she was wonderfully fluent in Spanish. She was often the one who went outside to learn what had happened. The three of us would follow her. After the shots died down and the street grew quiet again, people from the nearby homes and apartments poured out onto the corner, but nobody talked much. When the police came, it grew quieter still.

People were afraid because the shootings were gang related. Sometimes their own children were involved. People were scared, too, because of their lack of documentation. They were trying to keep a low profile. Nobody knew anything. Nobody talked. After the police had left the scene, helicopters circled low over the neighborhood searching for the perpetrators. They directed their high beam lights into the alleys, behind the garages, between the houses, and underneath the foliage—into *our* yard, behind *our* garage, underneath *our* bushes. The insistent moving beams of light created ominous shadows on the walls of my tiny room. Sometimes when I lay in my warm bed, trying to sink into a sleep that would not come, I pictured a frightened young man hiding somewhere in the bushes crouching low for cover—shivering, cowering, and vulnerable.

I was scared sometimes, not so much for myself, but because I knew the shots were meant to kill and that some young person might have lost his life or the use of his limbs to senseless violence. The young men in the gangs had to be afraid at times—or else they were stoned senseless. Every one of them knew someone who had been killed or maimed. They were so young—fifteen, sixteen, no one older than twenty. These gang members and their "wannabe" friends were really just teenagers, but their eyes were like steel, totally lifeless. I had never seen eyes like this before—not on human beings. I had a doll with eyes like that when I was a child—dark, staring, unblinking eyes. I think that's why I didn't play with her; there was nobody inside. It's your soul that shines out your eyes, I think. I wondered what these young men had done to their souls.

After a while I began to wonder if the gunshots that I heard at night were real or if I imagined them. Maybe I had just come to expect the cracks and pops of gunfire throughout the night. My body sensor was set now on hyper-alert, always tensed for action. I wondered if war was like this, if this was how one acquired post-traumatic stress syndrome. What if one *had* to live here—not by choice, as I did? I could get out when I wanted, but my neighbors—it was their world; it was their life; it was all that they could afford.

In August 1993, a young man was killed in the apartment behind our house. First we heard the gunshots and then the sirens—a loud wail of imminent danger that cut to silence when it neared our house. We rushed to the back corner to find out what had happened. The boy, Carlos Ramirez, was sixteen years old. He had lived in that apartment building with his family. His brother had been killed in a gang fight two years before. His girlfriend was pregnant with his child. It was beastly hot that night and when we went back inside I opened my bedroom windows wide. Carlos' mother was wailing and screaming. Her upstairs apartment window couldn't have been more than fifty feet from my own. I listened to her there in the dark, feeling empty, sad, and helpless. After an hour or two she became quiet, but I didn't sleep at all.

CHAPTER SIX

Life…what life? Life is nice but sometimes to me it's worthless. I'm already twenty and I feel like I ain't getting nowhere. When everybody is out there, I'm stuck inside a box.

—Victor Martinez

After Carlos Ramirez was shot and killed behind our house, I thought about the young people in our neighborhood every day. At night I either dreamed about them or else I was awakened by gunshots that alerted me to their violence. I slept, but never peacefully. My days and nights blurred into a state of perpetual preoccupation and worry. I wanted to learn as much I could about the plight of the young gang members—the toughs who hung out on the streets and their "women"—the girls in their midteens who had become mothers too soon.

Once the guys dropped out of school, they would party all day, drinking, cruising about if they had wheels, and planning their gang strategies—drug sales, thefts, and retaliation against their rivals. But the girls, the teen mothers, were more isolated. When they left school, they lived like prisoners in their cramped apartment units. With no access to automobiles and no job skills, they joined the ranks of full-time childcare providers at an early age. The *telenovelas,* the Spanish equivalent of the American soap operas, were their chief source of stimulation.

These young women were emotionally dependent on their boyfriends—even when the men had little to offer them but put-downs and the back of a hand. The girls emerged from time to time pushing baby strollers—to the market, the laundromat, the doctor. They used their strollers like the homeless use shopping carts, stacking them with purchases and the necessities of the day, until the babies almost disappeared. After a while, I stopped seeing flowers and color, blue sky and green trees. All I could see about me were the young people—hopeless, stuck, and in trouble.

Whenever I had the opportunity, I talked to them. I accosted youth on the streets, in the supermarket, in fast food restaurants, and at car washes. Wherever I found a young person working at a bottom level job or just hanging about, I asked the same questions over and over again, seeking to understand his life.

"Are you still going to school?" I asked a young man at the car wash one day.

"No, I dropped out."

"Do you think that you'll finish your high school diploma someday?"

A shrug of the shoulders.

"How old are you?"

"Eighteen"

"Do you have children?"

"Yeh, one, a little boy. He's got my name."

"Do you have a dream about what you would like to be doing five years from now?"

"Not really."

I just listened—collecting data, hardly conscious that I was doing so.

I met a lot of dead end kids. I had no temptation to lecture these young people about the importance of education or the impossibility of supporting a family on a minimum wage salary. I had no solutions to offer because I didn't understand the circumstances of their lives or why it was that they had no dreams. I couldn't comprehend the culture of poverty or the complex factors that permitted them to leave school without graduating and hang out on the streets all day.

These aimless young people were all over the city. Chronic poverty belched them out into the gutters of life and they were left there as human refuse. The mainstream support systems rolled on without them, filling their ranks with those who had an ounce of motivation, tenacity, or family support to sustain them. When those who dropped out of school turned eighteen, they disappeared from institutional radar screens. It no longer mattered to anyone whether they showed up on time, whether they earned credits toward a diploma, whether they succeeded or failed in their endeavors. Legally, the school system no longer had responsibility for them. They had had their chance at an education; they had been tried and found wanting. Now they were technically adults—in charge of their own pursuits but without the skills needed to build a sustainable future.

Their parents were chiefly Spanish speakers who worked long hours at grueling, minimum wage jobs to support their families. And because their parents had no experience in navigating adolescent rites of passage in these strange borderlands, they were often ill prepared to guide their troubled offspring into the future. And the young people, most of whom were second-generation immigrants, no longer looked to their parents as models. They formed their own rules for rules for loyalty, honor, duty, and acculturation. They mentored each other—often by way of the gang.

Only those who had served time in jail were accountable; they were wards of the criminal justice system. Their probation officers supervised their compliance and tried to steer their charges in the right direction. But the caseworkers in the Probation Department had big caseloads and couldn't afford to spend too much time with any one kid; they couldn't hold their hands. With the high dropout rate in the city and the rough gang environment, there were far too many young people on the streets who were footloose, undereducated, and unskilled. It was a recipe for trouble.

Oscar was one of the first young men who shared his story with me. He was eighteen years old and had been incarcerated six times—always for gang involvement and drug use. He had never met his father and his mother, who had been arrested for peddling drugs, was now in state prison. Oscar had no siblings. Each time he was released from jail, he stayed with the families of his friends as long as they would keep him or else he lived on the streets. He hadn't finished high school and he had no job skills. Oscar had absolutely no support system, no proper guides, no one to care for him when he was sick. It didn't seem to matter to anyone whether he lived or died and heroin had become his best friend. Oscar had raised himself and he was spiraling downward, lost in a dark, whirling pool of drugs and petty theft. He was dying before he'd had a chance to live.

Oscar introduced me to two of his friends, both of whom were on probation for gang activity and drug possession. They weren't going to school either. Once they had dropped out, it was hard to get back into the system—or to even want to. They were looking for employment, but who would hire them? They looked like trouble. The sadness of these young men haunted me. And once they were in my daily consciousness, they invaded my dreams as well. There was a look about these young people who had given up on themselves. They were joyless, tentative, defensive, guarded, hungry.

I had often prayed for the poor and the destitute, aware that I lived a life of privilege and that I lacked for nothing. I had prayed for the young men that I had been reading about in the newspaper—those who were killed or maimed through gang violence. Now, those for whom I had been praying were no longer anonymous. I began to know their names and faces. The lessons that I was learning were direct and personal and the youth and the neighborhood were my teachers.

Decades ago Father Flanagan, the founder of Boys' Town, discovered hurting young men on the Nebraska plains. In the aftermath of World War I and the Flu Epidemic of 1918, Flanagan met numerous men and boys whose lives were wasting away because of alcohol, poverty, and the ravages of war and disease. He opened a kind of flop-house for men where they could sober up and clean up—but boys began to come too—those who were orphaned because of the war or sickness, those whose families had fallen apart through adversity, and those who had no home to call their own. One day, the older men, chronic alcoholics, took Flanagan aside and told him to throw his lot with the youth.

"It's too late for us," they cautioned, "but it's not too late for the young ones. Don't worry about us. Work with them."

Flanagan heeded their advice.

"It was not too late for the boys," he said, "if someone were willing to take trouble about them and for them. Reconstruction of a man *(or woman!)*—the salvaging of a soul—was like any other repair job on earth. It had to begin on time, before decay had eaten too deep, before the clay had hardened into some irreversible shape. It had to begin when a man was still a boy."[1]

Most of the tough-looking kids on the streets of Santa Ana weren't old enough or experienced enough to be hardened criminals. But they were on a path to destruction and many had already created a paper trail that would follow them for the rest of their lives, identifying them as gang members and criminals. At seventeen, eighteen, nineteen, many of them had acquired criminal records and more than a few were branded as felons.

I brooded over these young people. It was intolerable for me to continue to live amongst them and watch their destruction, and so a plan gradually began to take shape within me. Its power was stronger than any obstacle put in its path. I was convinced that these young people in Santa Ana needed a place that they could call their own—a safe haven where they would be welcomed with dignity and grace no matter how much they had messed up in the past. I wanted them to have a refuge to count on when they were released from jail so that if they were resolved to better their lives, they would have the opportunity to do so.

And so with no experience whatsoever and with no certain knowledge that there was support for my plan, or indeed that my plan would work at all, I set out to find a building that we could use for a youth center and the funding that we would need to get started.

I didn't want to develop a traditional "drop out center," a ratty, weary storefront, where the young dregs of society could flop on second-hand couches and trade their tales of woe. I imagined a vital and stimulating environment where young people would be challenged to learn, to grow, to stretch, and finally, at long last, to dream. This program, which in my heart I began to call Taller San Jose in honor of St. Joseph, the patron of workers, was in some sense my birth child. My passion to have this program in the city was so strong that it was inconceivable to me that it would not be born. When naysayers cautioned me that it would take two to three years of planning to develop such an ambitious project, I countered, "If God can create a human being in nine months, why can't we get a program for youth up and running in that same time? These kids are dying on the streets. They need help now."

All that was lacking was will. I had lots of will. In fact, I had grown fierce in my resolve to get this program up and running. Like Abraham's wife Sarah and Mary's cousin Elizabeth, two women from Scripture who were past the prime of their child-bearing years, I, too, longed to give life to others—especially to the most vulnerable. I had a lot of love that had not yet been spent. What I hadn't counted on was that this birthing of Taller San Jose—the labor and the childbearing, as well as the child rearing, though immensely rewarding, might also be painful.

The first gift that God sent me on this new and determined journey was Dominic Walsh. Dominic was everything that I wasn't. He was a New Yorker by birth and culture; he was a skilled architect with striking good looks and he was half my age. When I first met him, he had just spent a year in a local Catholic seminary program, after which he had decided that the priest-hood was not his calling. Nevertheless, he had stayed in the neighborhood heading up a building project at the local Catholic school. Local gang members were his labor force and he had their trust.

Dominic had some valuable work experience and the worldly skills that I lacked. While I viewed him as a strong asset in the building of Taller San Jose, his brusque manner put me off at first. He played his cards close to his chest. He used words sparingly and to the point. Dominic preferred stares, grunts, and snorts to straightforward verbal communication. With a subtle shift of the eyes he could express either affirmation or disap-proval. Not unlike a number of his Irish forbears, Dominic was neither spontaneous nor effusive. Over time though, as I began to know him better, I learned to interpret his state of "neutral" as contentment and to discern the slightest upward curve of his lips as genuine delight. What we held in common and passed back and forth to each other on cue was hope for the young people of the city.

When I told Dominic about my dream, he bought in for the long haul and put all of his energy and brilliance behind the endeavor. And so we made a splendid team—a budding architect empowered by confidence and a fierce and seasoned nun burning with generativity.

Dominic brought a number of his gang friends to one of our early planning meetings. Junior, the most articulate among them, was the spokesperson for the group. Junior talked about his dream to finish school and the hope that one day he would get a good job and be able to support his family. Three months later, Junior was shot in a gang altercation. The bullet lodged in his spine, paralyzing him from the waist down. Junior now joined the company of other isolated young men—gunned down in the prime of life—who occupied small back bedrooms in over-crowded apartments, their bodies mangled and their souls twisted with plots for revenge. The tragedy of this senseless violence intensified my drive and vision.

Dominic and I stepped up our efforts and met with anyone who could guide our path. A local probation officer provided us with advice that was critical to our planning efforts. Street gangs claimed the majority of the neighborhoods in the city. Each of these areas, which comprised the poorest real estate in the city, was turf for a gang. Rival gang members could not cross certain streets without the threat of hostility breaking out. If we wanted to serve a broad range of young people and didn't want to identify ourselves with one gang to the exclusion of others, then we would have to locate our program in gang neutral territory. It was a challenge to find such a site. The neighborhoods in the city that were not claimed by gangs—the few upscale areas—weren't about to open their doors to potential trouble.

We looked at numerous building sites—a Quonset hut, a former mortuary, a windowless basement. All of them were both costly and unsatisfactory and none were in safe neighborhoods. And so we waited. When I began to despair, it was Dominic's stamina and doggedness that sustained my spirits.

When we did find a building, in the Civic Center area— with the police department six blocks to the west and the probation department four blocks to the east—we knew the hand of God was upon it. No gang wanted to claim this law enforcement domain; it was rare neutral ground, a demilitarized zone of the city. The proud, old building was once used as a Sunday school but had been used as county offices for the past several decades. Little had been done to maintain it and after years of neglect, it was in a wretched condition. Still, I was ecstatic to think that it could be ours. Early one morning while negotiations for the property hovered precariously between the county and city governments, we brought a small shovel, dug into the earth, and planted a medal of St. Joseph there to watch over the proceedings until the property was safely delivered into our hands.

While we waited for the complexities of the real estate agreement to be completed, the gang troubles in the city escalated.

Many people believe that entering and leaving gang life is a matter of choice—a decision and an act of will, but I have learned that it is much more complex than that. The gangs are Mafia-like in their structure—powerful and punishing. The gang proposes to be family and fellow gang members value loyalty to the point of death. Sometimes members who want to leave the benevolent stranglehold of the gang are jumped out, beaten by their peers and officially declared dead. This brutal rite of passage, which releases them from the gang's hold, protects them from the designation of traitor and frees them to pursue other paths. But rival gangs don't always get this message, and enemies have long memories. Once a young person has been labeled as a gang member, his life is in jeopardy. Some gang members begin to see the true nature of their existence—the trap that holds them in its punishing grasp.

What once enamored them becomes less attractive; they see it for what it is—and isn't. And so without formally announcing a change of status, they coexist within the gang while letting themselves be drawn more deeply into family or school or work. Over time, the primary allegiance to the gang no longer holds the same weight as before. Once a gang member has a child to support and a full-time job, he can sometimes ease out of the gang through benign neglect. But it isn't easy. You don't throw your friends away overnight and your enemies still know your name.

When Arturo Burgoa, a former gang member, spent six months in the county youth facility, he believed that his homeboys or *homies* would support him in this harrowing journey.

"But I never got letters from my friends," he said. "When you're locked up it's as if you were dead. They forget about you. When you're down, they want to put you in the ground. In the end, it was my mother who came to visit me."

Gang members don't leave their past behaviors behind because of one "Scared Straight" pep talk. A straightforward presentation about prison life may set them to thinking about their choices, but in the end, it is the power of trusting relationships that counts the most. When one leaves "the family," one needs to know that there is someone to move toward, that one is not going to find himself naked and lonely in the middle of the street. It is not in the nature of an adolescent to stand alone without peers, without protection.

I have never pretended to understand the complexity of gang culture but I don't negate it. It is quite real and young men and women have lost their lives in its service. I do know about human dignity though, and I believe that the young people with whom we would be working deserved to be treated with respect regardless of their misdeeds. I knew that both education and employment would be essential elements in helping young people to achieve a sense of self-worth. Violence reigned on the mean streets of Santa Ana and in its varied and subtle forms, it crept into the apartments and homes as well, sometimes pitting family members against each other. I wasn't arrogant or self-assured enough to pretend that we could solve all the problems that flow from gangs and violence. The only real weapon that we would have was love. I believe that love, soft and strong, gentle yet potent—has the power to prevail over evil.

In a cruel twist of fate, in December 1994, negotiations for the lease of our building broke down. Orange County declared bankruptcy, the first county in the history of the country to do so. All fiscal transactions, including the lease of our building, were put on hold for nearly a year and we were powerless to intervene. Powerlessness is the lot of the poor—no money, no clout, no voice, no influence. The poor are experienced in waiting and in settling for less than they need or want, but I wasn't and I seethed with a holy impatience. But there was nothing that I could do but to take a number and stand in line. The future site for Taller San Jose was just six blocks from our old gray corner house and so nearly every weekend I walked over to touch it, to claim it with my heart, and to keep the dream alive within me.

⚬⚬⚬

There were sixty-four homicides in Santa Ana that year—fifty-nine of them were designated as gang related. During the interminable nine month wait to clear the county's shameful financial dealings, more young teens claimed a gang for the first time; some were brutally wounded; others went to jail and *veteranos,* those experienced in the ways of crime, left the prison system and spilled back onto the streets to recruit and coach the newcomers.

Finally, in September 1995, the building issue resolved, we opened the Taller San Jose program. The long-coveted building was weary, dilapidated, and achy in the joints, but it couldn't have been in a more perfect location. We coaxed eight imperfect young people off the street with promises of pizza and tamales, and as a new staff, fragile and flawed ourselves, we began to listen to their stories and to learn from them.

⚬⚬⚬

Susana, eighteen, had left school when she was fourteen and no force in the world could have budged her back into the system. At school, in her small circle of friends, she had been young and in love, rejected and cast aside, publicly humiliated by her boyfriend and his cronies, lied to. She stayed at home nursing her hurts in shame. She hadn't meant to back off forever but she never found her way back to school. For four years, she cowered inside and hid in the safety of her house investing only in trusted familial relationships. While she chose isolation and protection to solve her problems, stagnation came with the package. She was a child in a woman's body.

"I was like a housewife," she said of those years. "I cooked and cleaned and took care of children."

Manuel, nineteen, sought safety, too. He was slight of build and slow to learn. He didn't really want to join the neighborhood gang, but he was of the right age and he was bullied into claiming one side or the other. He witnessed unspeakable crimes and was threatened into silence. He was beaten and bruised and was very much afraid. So he had stopped going to school and he hid, working with his father when there was work to do. But his voice had been stilled, his development stunted, and now he could only utter monosyllables in response to the simplest queries. The real Manuel, the man the boy was meant to be, was buried someplace deep within.

Raul, eighteen, had just left the jail. He had been arrested for aggravated assault related to a gang incident. Raul's father had a drug business and had cycled in and out of prison for twenty years, dragging his family ever deeper into unrelenting poverty. Raul, the oldest male in the family, had no effective male model. Like any kid his age, he sought identity and meaning through love, power, affiliation, trust, and respect. With his father in prison and his mother working two and three jobs, his family offered little structure and support. But the gang promised to meet all of Raul's needs. The gang offered him a sense of duty, responsibility and a chain of command, punishments, rewards, and rites of passage. In his allegiance to the gang Raul found a sense of belonging that he had craved. He was scared though. The gang also instructed him in the ways of violence and he lived in constant terror.

We were an unseasoned staff and in the beginning there was much to be done. We cared for the grim old building as if it were a palace, but no matter how much we cleaned, it looked weary— a setting for minor public officials in the Ukraine. I was determined that, even its abject state, the building would have dignity. Transient drug dealers had a long-time habit of sleeping on the second floor landing each night. In our first weeks, before they relocated their sleeping quarters elsewhere, I had the privilege of picking up their used condoms as I climbed the stairs in the mornings. Better me than the students, I judged.

No one on the staff had significant experience in working with gang members and their issues. The young people who walked in the door challenged our readiness to meet their needs. Our hope and fervor sometimes took the form of anxiety; our inexperience cloaked itself in angst. Sometimes we wrestled with each other regarding our mission and who we could best serve and how. One staff member was adamantly opposed to accepting kids in the program who were currently involved in gang activity. She felt that we were naïve and not prepared to work with them. She asserted that by admitting them to the program, we jeopardized the safety of other students.

"They have to go some other place first," she insisted.

But there was no other place. There were only the streets. We had to learn how to work with whoever walked in the front door and we had to find that path by walking.

CHAPTER SEVEN

All my life I've been taking chances…bad chances.
—Ramon Padilla

It was unthinkable to me that I would miss my own mother's death, but that's what happened. It was my sister, Maureen, who was at my mother's side when she left the shell of her weary body behind. I was in Philadelphia at a nuns' conference when my sister called me to tell me that my mother had suffered a heart attack. I knew immediately that she wouldn't live. She'd changed in the last year of her life. Her soul force had withered, receding from the lifelong vibrancy that I'd known within her. I'd noticed the marked change the previous Thanksgiving when I'd gone to pick her up for the family celebration. Although I'd seen her not two weeks before, in that brief lapse of time some silent and invisible diminishment had visited itself upon her. From that day forward I called her everyday. I knew there would soon be a last call, a last visit, some last words.

After her death, I grieved my mother terribly. My dad had died twenty years before and in the past two decades I'd grown to know my mother differently than I'd known her as a child. She transferred to me the vulnerability that she'd once shared with my father, humbly endearing herself to me. Toward the end of her life I felt for the first time that she needed me and I wanted her to need me. I felt useful.

The day after my mother's funeral, I went down to the ocean to walk in the waves. I couldn't bear to be hugged or even touched by the kindest words. And so alone, I walked back and forth between the Seal Beach pier and the jetty, hour after hour, letting the waves lap at my ankles, mingling my tears with the foamy tide.

It wasn't long after my mother's death that I adopted Our Lady of Guadalupe as my mother. I had never before been a great fan of the Virgin Mary. It wasn't that I didn't believe that Mary was the Mother of God or that I didn't hold her in high esteem, but when I was young she seemed an impossible model to follow—a woman without sin, who had successfully resisted all temptations and who had not one blemish upon her spotless soul.

And so I'd set the Virgin Mary aside for decades—in a kind of reverential niche—until I was in desperate need of her. When my mother died, it was the brown-skinned *morenita* who was waiting to embrace me—the simple indigenous woman who had appeared to the Indian, Juan Diego, over four centuries before in Mexico. The dark-skinned Virgin had spoken to Juan Diego in tender words. *"Mijo,"* she had called him—my son. She had sent him to the local bishop to beg for a church to be built and she had filled his *tilma* with roses in December to add credibility to his message. She had promised to be with her people—the neglected and the poor—at all times and everywhere no matter how abject their circumstances.

Now, as I took the Virgin of Guadalupe to be my mother, I proclaimed her to be the patroness of Taller San Jose, too, and of all the young people who would ever enter its doors. I knew that whatever the circumstances of their lives, they could use a heavenly advocate who understood what it was to be Mexican and to be poor and to have the fierce love of a mother on your side.

In the days, weeks, months that I grieved my mother, I was grateful that my time was filled with demanding tasks—the physical cleaning of the Taller San Jose building, the loading and unloading of used furnishings, the networking with educational partners throughout the city, and the constant learnings about life on the streets and the power of the gang culture. I was grateful to the first young people who came to the door and who trusted us with their lives. I was eager to hear their stories and to learn from them. My mother was safe on the other side. She didn't need me anymore. I was happy that somebody did.

After my mother's death, Ramon Padilla was one of the first young men to stop by my office to offer me his condolences. The bulk of his presence took up all the light in my office doorway. It was hard not to notice Ramon Padilla. It wasn't just his physical presence that overpowered a room. Ramon had a big soul and wherever he landed, his energy spilled out and over, catching everyone into a warm inclusive puddle. But that's only if he let you know him.

Ramon had a darker side, too. He could turn mean in an instant and throw a look meant to chill—or kill. Ramon had served time in prison and he knew how to protect himself. But Ramon was soft with me. He felt safe at Taller San Jose and slowly he let his guard down. In bits and pieces he told me his story—or the parts he thought a nun could handle. He told me of the long gutter-run of drugs, how low he'd fallen. He hadn't just dropped out of school. He had dropped out of life for nearly a decade and almost killed himself along the way.

"I guess it started when I was a kid and they put me in the dummy class," he said. "I didn't learn fast, but I didn't wanna be in no dummy class. Everyone could see you go in and out of the dummy bungalow, so I just left. I was eleven, maybe twelve. My parents were at work all day so even though they dropped me off at school, I didn't stay. Nobody could keep me there. I just wouldn't go."

Ramon told me then about how he wandered home each day with some like-minded friends and began to hang out in the park. They started sniffing glue. One day, a friend who was just a year older than he was brought a whole stash of marijuana to the scene. Ramon had been watching the older guys taking hits for quite a while and he wanted to be like them. He was more than ready to advance to the next level and to prove himself. When he did go to school, it was to sell weed. The rest of the day, he just got high and drank, waiting for someone to beat up or rob.

The first time Ramon got in trouble with the law he had been acting as a lookout, watching for homeowners or undercover cops as the more experienced guys staged a robbery. He was the one who was appointed to whistle when there were signs of trouble and to signal again when the coast was clear. He was thirteen years old when he landed in juvenile hall for the first time. He never did go to school again regularly after that. The gang encircled him. They gave the marching orders and issued the code of behavior to follow. The gang signaled what clothes to wear, the hand signs to make, the placement of tattoos. They even gave Ramon a special name to formalize his acceptance among them. They called him *Oso*, Spanish for bear.

"The first time I was in juvie," Ramon said, "I sat on this hard steel bench waiting to be booked. There was this girl there too and everybody, all the inmates and guards, knew her name and called out to her. And she knew all of them, too. I thought that was cool. I wanted to be like her—important."

Ramon told me how he had progressed from one drug to the next over nearly a decade—first crystal meth and then cocaine and heroin. He came to know each of the drugs well, how much to take, and when and where to exercise caution.

By the time he was eighteen he had become a transient, finding temporary quarters with his druggie friends or living on the streets.

"I looked horrible," he admitted. He only had the clothes on his back and he didn't take care of himself. He wasn't any good at selling drugs, so he stole instead. Every day he needed more money for a fix.

"For years, I was so stoned that it was all black out time," he told me. "Most of the time, I don't remember what I did."

"When you were on the streets," I asked, "what did you do at night? Where did you sleep?"

"There weren't any nights," he said, unblinking.

"Oh," I said and said no more. I began to grasp the frantic degradation of it all.

⚜

Between eighteen and twenty-three, Ramon spent much of his time behind bars. First it was the men's jail. He grew used to that. But when he was sent to state prison—Wasco, Soledad, Vacaville—the rules changed. There, the prisoners were in charge.

"You could feel people looking at you as you got off the bus," he said. "Eyeing you...sizing you up. I'll never forget arriving at Soledad in the rain. As long as I live I'll never forget that gray day and the rain." Only the tough survived the rapes, beatings, and murders in the prison system.

⚜

When he wasn't serving time, Ramon worked, but only to buy drugs and he had a hard time holding onto a job. He was always stoned—either hyped up from cocaine or crystal meth or lethargic from the soothing heroin. He knew the employers were on to him. They didn't want him around and none of his jobs lasted long.

Although Ramon thought he was savvy and careful about his drug use, he wasn't careful enough. One night his right arm swelled up to the size of a pumpkin and he was delirious with pain. Desperate and afraid, he begged his friends to take him to an emergency room.

The ER nurse eyed his tough looks and the collapsed veins in his arms and legs.

"Are you using drugs?" she asked accusingly.

He nodded a fateful yes.

When the test results came back, without a hearing before either judge or jury, Ramon, now twenty-four years old, received a damning life sentence. He learned that he had Hepatitis C, a chronic disease that attacked his liver and made him weak and tired. He also learned that Hepatitis C was a highly contagious disease and that for the rest of his life he would have to take responsibility for not passing it on to others—including future sexual partners.

"I'm the only one responsible," he admits when he tells his story. "Nobody made me do it. I put the needle in my arm."

Learning about his disease was his lowest moment.

"That's when I wanted to die, and I tried. One day I just loaded up, hoping I would go out on one big high, but it didn't work," he said. "I was stuck with myself."

⤙⤙⤜

Ramon is off the streets now and living with his parents.

"I'm an adult now—way past eighteen," he says. "I shouldn't be living with my parents anymore, but I'm thankful that they are there to help me to get on with my life."

It was his mother who told him about Taller San Jose.

"I told her that I didn't need to come here—that I could get better and stay clean on my own, but I couldn't."

Ramon is still working on his high school diploma but his mind doesn't work the way it used to. He knows that he's not stupid, but he can't remember things. He can't concentrate.

"I don't know if I never could learn or if I fried my brain with drugs," he laments.

He picks up odd jobs for pocket money and he's embarrassed about not holding a real job. He doesn't feel like a man.

Step by step though, he's cleaning up his life. Last year he voluntarily surrendered and served time in jail to clear up an outstanding warrant so that he could get his driver's license. He'd been driving for years without one.

Still fragile, he clings to Taller San Jose like a miraculous buoy thrown out upon his sea of troubled waters. He has a new set of friends that he's met there—friends who don't drag him down. There's a certain emotional clumsiness about Ramon. At times he is twenty-five going on fourteen. The drugs took away his boy-to-man growing up years.

"All my life I've been taking chances," he says, "bad chances. Now I'm trying to take good chances and make right decisions. I still make mistakes, but I try to not make the mistakes I used to make in the past. Like I don't go to the old neighborhood because I know there's always something going on there that's bad news for me. I can't take that chance. It will only lead me to a place I don't want to go no more."

※※※

When Ramon joined Taller San Jose's writers' circle he began to find his voice. The group meets twice a month at the Sisters' Motherhouse in Orange. The format is simple.

"Just write what you don't want to forget," I counsel the writers. "There'll be no pressure to read what you write. Go wherever your soul takes you."

Nobody ever writes about geraniums or sunshine or what happened on their summer vacation. The writers simply tell their stories, beg to be heard.

I'm not perfect and I still make mistakes, wrote Ramon one day, *but now I'M the one who deals with them. Before I came to Taller San Jose, I was trying to kick off Meth. I had just quit a job that I was lucky to find—a good job. Who could ask for anything more?*

I was on a roll—one month clean and sober and that was a long time for me. When I had a few checks in the bank, I started to get high again and then I went downhill—fast. I didn't want to work no more, so I quit. A month passed and I was back to my old self—NO MONEY, NO JOB...A GOOD FOR NOTHING DRUG ADDICT!

I didn't want to live no more, but I didn't want to start living on the streets again. I knew where that was going to take me. I decided to try to get my high school diploma. I've had my ups and downs but

I've made a positive choice for myself and I've told myself to get my education and to stay away from drugs and alcohol. So far I've been doing pretty good. I'm not free yet...but who says I can't get there? I know there's a future for me and I'm going out to get it.

When he finished reading what he had written, he went on to talk about the burden of Hepatitis C, how it had changed his life forever, skewing his sense of well-being.

"I can't even have sex," he acknowledged, "without telling some girl first. It'll be like that forever."

A quiet appreciation followed Ramon's sharing. Nods of approval. Gratitude for his testimony.

Later when we came downstairs and joined the nuns in the cafeteria food line, Ramon and the others piled food high on their trays.

"Hey, Sister Eileen," one of the young men leaned over and whispered in my ear. "That was like church up there today, wasn't it?"

"Yeh." Indeed, the writing *was* like church—the sacred quiet time, the visit to one's soul, the reverent reading, the affirmations, the confessions of wrongs done, and the tacit forgiveness of us all.

⊱✦⊰

Ramon has so many hurdles in life to overcome—to stay clean and sober, to hold on to his dignity and self-worth even though he is not yet the man he wants to be, to avoid the traps of the old neighborhood and the old friendships that can drag him back onto the streets. I'm never certain how it is that I can help Ramon, but I do care deeply about him and I can listen. And I promise him my prayers.

I'm never certain exactly what I mean when I tell someone that I will pray for them. Prayer is not magic, I know. But I do promise to keep that person in my heart and to say their name before God often. My best model for intercessory prayer is based on the story of an elderly monk with chronically bad feet. He had grumbled and complained repeatedly and asked God to spare him this chronic affliction. Having said it all over and over again, he now simply knelt in the back of the church each day and voiced his petition in two words—"God, feet."

That's how I pray for Ramon. I say "God, Ramon." It's an act of trust. It's all I know to do.

CHAPTER EIGHT

I do not want to be rewarded for the things I have done with my life. I want to be rewarded for the way my life has changed.

—Juan Carrasco

You can't paint and worry at the same time. That's why I started doing watercolors. At first my paintings were safe and tentative, but recently they've grown bolder and brighter. I paint whatever appeals to me—big loose flowers are favorites, but I've painted Our Lady of Guadalupe too, and from time to time I paint the faces of students at Taller San Jose—trying to capture the hope or hopelessness that they carry within them. The cast of the eyes, the slack of the mouth, or the set of a chin—each feature can reveal determination, despair, desolation, or confidence.

I can't worry while I'm painting because the process requires that I focus all of my attention on the object in front of me and that I am present to the moment. I'm a "wet" painter. I like the effect of two colors merging quickly on damp paper. Wet watercolorists work fast and by instinct. We don't have a lot of control over the finished product, instead we rely on imagination and trust.

I am often disappointed in my paintings. I want to paint better and with greater ease, but then I am often amazed that I can paint at all. Even when my paintings don't turn out well, it is good for me to stay with the process and to paint often. The repeated experience reinforces within me the magic of mixing colors and the techniques that can make a painting vital. While I'm no longer a beginning painter, there is still much that I don't know how to do and sometimes I get discouraged. While I stay within my range of experience, I also push insistently at the outer edges of my craft.

Painting is kind of an analogy for my work at Taller San Jose. I think that if we don't experiment there and push the outer edges, risking some mistakes, then we have a safe, flat program that really doesn't address the issues of the students. It's easier to manage something safe and flat. I just don't think that's what we're supposed to be doing. The young people bring their lives to us—trusting that in this narrow window of opportunity we can point the way to hope.

Like painting, Taller San Jose is deeply engaging to me, but not exactly relaxing. It's the perfectionist in me, I think, that gets frustrated. I want everyone to succeed. I want everything to work out the first time around. I have a patience with people, however, that I don't have with paint.

I've learned to view each young person as a work of art—created as God meant them to be, whole and worthy in themselves in spite of their mess-ups and regrets. I think that my role is to help young people believe in themselves. I want them to understand that in calling them into life, God did not make a mistake.

Yolanda Castro isn't a mistake, but she's made a lot of them in life and she can be so down on herself at times that I'm the one who's had to hold the hope for her. Her life has been so tough that she's not convinced that God loves her, cares for her, or even that she was meant to be. In the meantime, I can love her to the best of my ability, hoping that one day she'll find the strength to value herself.

The first time I met Yolanda Castro she was in the career center. One of the volunteers had asked me to keep an eye on her. She told me that Yolanda was needy, had led a rough life, and needed a mentor who would be steady and strong. Yolanda got me instead. Our relationship was hit and miss for several months. Yolanda was an on-again, off-again student. She was rarely there.

Yolanda's mother left her when she was six weeks old. Her mother, who had been on heroin, no longer wanted a predictable family life. So Yolanda grew up without a mom. Her father, who earned his living as a gardener, provided for his two young girls the best he could, but he worked long hours and the girls were looked after by others.

Yolanda was always a restless soul, filled with passion and energy. She had a hard time concentrating in school. Sometimes I've wondered if she entered the world a "drug baby," affected by her mother's heroin use before she was born.

When Yolanda was thirteen, she took off with her boyfriend—not caring about school or her family. Her father cared though and reported her missing. It was the first time, but not the last, that she spent time in Juvenile Hall.

The next year she was pregnant. Yolanda was fifteen years old when she gave birth to her daughter, Wendy. Alone, and without a woman to guide her, childbirth was a traumatic experience. From that point on, Yolanda just bumped along—always dragging her little girl behind her even though in many ways she was just a child herself.

Yolanda's family was very poor and she was always desperate for money. Her father had put the press on her to find a job—after all, she spoke English, was young and strong, and had a child to support. She found jobs but none of them lasted long. Her behavior was erratic.

Yolanda had a very low opinion of herself. Still a teenager, she already proclaimed herself a victim, certain that from the beginning of time all the cards were stacked against her. She gave in easily to defeat and despair and when she was very low, it was impossible to comfort her. I could stand next to her. Sometimes when she was crying, she let me hold her, but all the holding was mine; her body was stiff and drawn inward.

❧

Just after Christmas one year, Yolanda called me from jail. She had been at the wrong place at the wrong time and with the wrong people. One of her drug-ridden friends had left his gun in her car. She was held responsible for it. It was, after all, her vehicle and her friend denied that it was his weapon.

I went to visit her one Sunday morning after Mass—or at least I tried to. I took a number with the myriad of other visitors to the women's jail that day. I was #376. I sat for three hours in the stark waiting room of the central jail. When my number was finally called, I was allowed into the visitor's area where Yolanda and I would be permitted to talk from behind a glass wall. I sat there another hour...waiting. Finally, an attendant motioned me over to a bulletproof booth and told me that Yolanda was on kitchen duty and that I would have to come another day.

I felt powerless, angry, and frustrated at the powers-that-be, at Yolanda, at poverty and its consequences.

I went home and wrote her a letter:

Dear Yolanda,

You asked me the other day if I thought you needed counseling? Yes, Yes, YES, I do. Not because you're crazy or because there is anything wrong with you but because you have a lot of hardships to deal with and you need someone to accompany you with those—not a social worker or case manager—somebody who just cares about YOU. I can help you find a counselor if you would like.

Yes, I worry about you because life out on the streets is hard. You're not in a good situation right now and you're around people who don't love you or even like you. That can make you put your hard edge on—and that is not all of who you are. You have a loving and warm person inside of you who wants to have a good life and to make a good life for your daughter.

I think that God gave you a strong inner core and that He will be there to support you. Don't be afraid. I know that you didn't have a mom and that's a big loss. A good mom can teach a girl how to grow up and how to love and to take care of herself. But you've got us here. We'll be brother and sister and mom to you until you're grown up and steady. I keep you in my heart, Preciosa, and I pray for you every day.

Sister Eileen

Dear Sister Eileen,

I don't belong in here but I'm not sad anymore. I'm afraid. Afraid to get released and to fail again. I want to be responsible like I used to be, before the devil disguised itself and ruined my life. The worst part is I don't realize when I start going wrong and then I can't get back on my feet. I have a weakness. I trust the wrong people. Have I ever told you that if it was up to me I'd rather die? I let my daughter down, Sister. I feel that my family could do a better job taking care of her. There's no bad influences there. As for my life, I come across bad all the time and I hate myself for that.

Yolanda

When Yolanda was released from jail, she came to see me and brought with her a gift certificate for one hundred and fifty dollars that I had given her for Christmas. It was for a shopping trip to buy work clothes for her and it was to be accompanied by a personal shopper. I tried to connect Yolanda with one of Taller San Jose's young, trendy staff members, but she wanted to go shopping with me. She asked if the offer was still good—after she had been to jail and messed up and everything. I assured her that it was, but that she had to hold a job for thirty days before we could spend it. We went to the thrift shop to get her some starter clothes.

Yolanda found her job and kept it. Thirty days later she called me and we made an appointment to go fashion shopping.

At the local Ross' store she piled the cart high with items. I screwed up my face and sucked in my breath whenever she chose leopard prints or dark slinky things. I kept pulling pink and white fluffy things off the rack. Sometimes I held my tongue; sometimes I chided her.

"You already have enough black clothes." I sounded like a mom. When we left the dressing room the hooker clothes were left behind.

Later, in the shoe store, a sassy young clerk eyed Yolanda's tough looks and said, "Are you from some shelter or something? Who's that lady with you? Is she your mom?" The sassy girl knew full well that we weren't related.

"She's my mom today," said Yolanda.

When we shared a sandwich afterward, we talked about which tattoo Yolanda would get removed first, which ones embarrassed her, which ones seemed to get in the way of her moving ahead in the job market.

I dropped her off at a hundred dense apartment buildings all sitting on top of each other. She gave me a hug and a kiss as she hopped out of the car with her shopping bags.

"She's my mom today," I repeated to myself all the way home. It was the day before Mother's Day. Yolanda did need a mom. I hoped that I knew how to be one.

❧❀❧

I didn't see Yolanda for several months and then one morning I received a desperate phone call from her. She was living out of her car in the parking lot outside of her father's apartment. He had kicked her out. She had her daughter with her and when the father went to work, they would go in and clean up. She asked me about a shelter. I'd talked with her before about a shelter where she could live with Wendy until she got her feet on the ground, but she'd never been seriously interested in this possibility. She was a restless soul.

"Shelters have rules," I reminded her, "and they'll test for drugs."

"I know," she whimpered through her tears.

I asked her if she could come in and see me. She told me that she looked too awful and she didn't want anybody to see her and that she didn't have any bus money.

"I'll be here all day," I told her. "I don't care how you look."

I encouraged her to call her social worker and ask for help. She was afraid to do so; she felt like a failure. I urged her again to call. She really needed housing and food. There was no way for me to call Yolanda back—she was calling from a pay phone on the corner.

When we hung up, I called Yolanda's social worker. She didn't answer so I left a message. I told her that I was worried about Yolanda and asked her to call me. It was Yolanda's business, though, to share the details of her life.

In the early afternoon, our office manager buzzed me to tell me that both Yolanda and her social worker were in the lobby.

I was relieved. The three of us met and the social worker got on the phone to find someplace for Yolanda to stay for awhile.

❧

Several weeks later there was a gentle knock at my door. I looked up to see Yolanda peering from around the corner. She was apologetic for not keeping in touch. Just the same, she hit me up for money. She needed it for a down payment on a room for rent.

"Just $50.00," she said. "I'll pay it back."

I didn't think I'd see the money again, but it didn't matter just then. She was sad, stringy, wiry. Not on drugs, I thought, or hoped. Just worn out and worried. She'd been crying. Her eyes glanced downward toward a painting that I had just completed. It was the face of a young Hispanic woman—no one in particular. I had just wanted to see if I could paint hopelessness.

Yolanda studied the painting as if she were looking in a mirror.

"Is that me?" she asked me. "That's what I look like, isn't it?"

"You're prettier than that," I answered, "but you do look very sad."

She told me then that she had just left her daughter, Wendy, with her father and her sister.

"I can't keep dragging her around with me," she said. "It's not good for her. She needs to be in school. I'm not good for her, Sister Eileen."

I silently agreed. I'd been with Yolanda a number of times when she was sad and depressed, crying with Wendy by her side. I wondered then how I would have felt, as a child, if I'd seen my mother so sad, so often, alone and in tears. I climbed inside Wendy's skin or tried to, and when I did, I felt terribly sad and dreadfully insecure.

"I've got to go," Yolanda said. "I've got to get this money to this woman by noon so that I can have the room." She was moving to Los Angeles. She didn't know anybody there, but she'd found a job picking up repossessed cars in a rough part of the city. The room was fifty dollars a week. I couldn't imagine what it looked like. But Yolanda wanted to get out of Santa Ana.

"There's only trouble for me here," she said.

I wondered what awaited her in Los Angeles.

"Let me pray for you," I said. I made the sign of the cross on her forehead and asked God to protect her and to look after her little daughter as well. Then we hugged goodbye and she was gone.

I loved this wayward child. I prayed for her every night as I closed my eyes and recited the words of a favorite psalm, *I waited patiently for the Lord; he inclined to me and heard my cry* (Ps 40:1). I cried out for both Yolanda and for myself. She was in so much pain. God had placed her in my life and I really didn't know how to help her.

I wasn't surprised when Yolanda called me a few weeks later to tell me how filthy Los Angeles was and how cruel her boss was to her. Moving to Los Angeles, she acknowledged, had been a big mistake. She was broke, alone, and very discouraged.

Still, her next call was upbeat and hopeful.

"Guess where I am?" Yolanda asked. I hoped it wasn't jail. I didn't think so; she wasn't crying. "Las Vegas." She answered before I had a chance to guess.

"What are you doing there?" I asked. I was half-afraid to hear the answer.

"Things were awful in Los Angeles," she said. "That place is the pits. The owner of that company was really mean. He yelled at us all. Everybody hated him. I couldn't do it anymore, but I met this girl who has family in Las Vegas and so she invited me to come with her. I'm going to find a job here and then I'll be able to send money back for Wendy."

My mother instinct clicked in strong.

"Las Vegas is a dangerous city," I said, sounding like some aged fuddy-duddy. "You take care of yourself. Don't get into trouble." I'd meant prostitution, but I didn't say the word aloud.

"I'll be okay," she assured me. "I just wanted to let you know where I was."

"I love you, *Preciosa*," I said.

"Yeh, me too…you," she answered.

When I did hear from her again, it was by way of a message left on my answering machine. Yolanda was in jail in Henderson, Nevada.

How I longed to surround Yolanda with the unconditional love of God—the security of knowing that no matter what she had done or might do, God chooses to love her all over again each morning. Sometimes it's hard for me to grasp how constant and all-embracing God's love can be. We humans are much quicker to write each other off. Last year, when I was in the mountains for several days, I kept taking pictures of the same mountain over and over again—at sunrise and sunset, in light and in shadow. I found the mountain incredibly beautiful. When my photos were finally developed, I had five or six prints of that same mountain peak. The photos all looked pretty much the same. But everyday, when I woke up, I had found the mountain beautiful all over again and I was eager to capture it anew. I think that is what the unconditional and all-embracing love of God must be like—every time God looks at me He is filled with wonder and delight, every time he looks at Yolanda, He is filled with wonder and delight.

While I hate the poverty that I see around me, the poverty that crushed Yolanda from her earliest days and left her soul bleeding and wounded, at the same time, I have come to understand what St. Francis of Assisi meant when he spoke of embracing Lady Poverty. Francis is talking about the vow of poverty that I took when I was twenty years old. Through this vow, I promised not to own or to covet worldly goods. I promised to live simply and to depend upon what would be provided to me. I also had the understanding that I would do the Lord's work and earn my keep and that I would help to support my sisters whatever their needs might be. I understand this vow of poverty better each day and I know that it is not just about *things* but also about the simplicity with which I comport myself in life. This vow of poverty also challenges my arrogance and it reminds me not to view myself as superior to anyone. But my vow refers to voluntary poverty, a spiritual self-chosen striving for simplicity of life. My soul has become sensitized to detachment, to purging myself of needless wants. If I ever feel the moment of want—it is because I choose to ignore a passing fancy or I do not honor a transitory whim—it's not about real deprivation. My voluntary vow of poverty has freed me to travel more lightly through life so that I can make myself available to others. At this point in my life, I have few strings that tie my heart to places, possessions, or persons. It hasn't always been that way; sometimes I have clung fiercely to a want or need. I have been held prisoner by a slender thread of desire.

But real poverty, the poverty that crushed Yolanda from the start, is ugly and powerful. When I am close to its grim reality, I always come away sad. Real poverty forces choices. Shall I pay the rent this month or shall I feed my child? Shall I try to finish my high school education or shall I take that bottom level factory job? Shall I pay the overdue light bill or shall I take my child to the doctor? The two dollars that I have—shall I put a gallon of gas in the car or shall I take the bus?

I can't imagine trying to explain my self-chosen vow of poverty to Yolanda or anyone else who lives in real want each day. It would be a pointless philosophical monologue. I wouldn't even try. I'm not poor—not really.

Last night I drove five students home from the beach. Each person gave me specific directions. "Turn here, stay to the right; turn left at the signal." Each one knew the contours of his or her neighborhood well. Each dwelling I stopped at was poorer than the last until we finally stopped at Luz Cervantes' apartment on Minnie Street, crowded quarters that she shared with seven other family members. Even in its state of semirehabilitation, Minnie Street is the bottom level of life in Santa Ana. People who live there cling to life by their fingernails—sometimes just a step away from homelessness. To me, the crowded aging apartments on Minnie Street are synonymous with crushing poverty. Afterward, I went home to my comfortable convent. I prayed for Yolanda and wondered where she was and how she was. I slept all though the night, but I awakened with dirty poverty in my mouth.

CHAPTER NINE

Memories are left from a fantasy that homies and I share...going to the park and chilling together, fighting against enemies, our foolish dreams, taking our families down...until pain.

—Tony Burgoa

Eddie Vargas was built like a bull. His large clean shaven head forged upward from his powerful neck and massive shoulders. I wouldn't have wanted to be on his bad side in a dark alley. Eddie was studying to pass his high school equivalency exam. He'd just spent several months in jail when he first came to Taller San Jose and he and his girlfriend had a little baby. His roots with the gang were still strong.

When Eddie knocked at my office door one morning, he didn't want to come in; he just wanted to say "good-bye and thank you" for all we'd done for him.

Not so fast.

"Where are you going and why?" I wanted to know.

"I need a job," he muttered. "I have to pay off my probation bills and my family needs help with the rent."

NO! I protested inside. *You can't go out there yet; you're not ready! You'll fall back into trouble!*

When he wasn't at Taller San Jose, Eddie would be with his friends, the gang—where else?

Eddie didn't have any skills or work experience, so he was going to go out and bust his buns for less than $6.00 an hour. I feared that he'd wear himself out in some menial job and then go out partying with his buddies to recover from the indignity of it all. In the meantime, he would abandon his studies and be back where he started from—which was nowhere—no skills, no education, a criminal record, and no way to grow.

Taller San Jose had served as a way station when he came out of jail, but it wasn't going to break the cycle of poverty—at least not for Eddie.

This was my first tip-off that some of our students needed immediate employment. They were dealing with day-to-day survival issues—food, shelter, and transportation. If we wanted to hold on to them longer at Taller San Jose, we were going to have to create a business and hire them ourselves.

That's how we started making benches. It was an informal arrangement at first, more of an experiment than a business. We had inherited over two hundred solid core pine doors from the Motherhouse of my religious congregation. The nuns were renovating two floors of the big central headquarters and they invited us to go through the building to see if there were any furnishings or shelves that might be helpful to us in renovating our building. I was looking at the lighter stuff—desks, tables, and chairs—but Dominic Walsh was marking all the doors. He and four of the Taller students loaded and unloaded the heavy doors on and off the truck.

"What on earth are you going to do with those?" I asked Dominic.

"You'll see," was all the answer that I got in return.

Dominic used the wooden doors to renovate the building and to construct starter desks. He used the doors to design and build shutters, table tops, light boxes, and chair railings. And then one day we slipped into designing benches.

Under Dominic's tutelage, Eddie and several of our other young male students began to create benches on their own. The first one looked okay, but it was pitched at an odd angle and when I sat on it, I slid to the floor. The next benches that they made were awkward—too big and too heavy — but over time they pared down the dimensions, creating pleasing designs with a unique California look. The more garden benches that the young men produced, the more income we brought in, and soon we actually were able to pay the workers.

The fact that the benches were made from convent doors was a big selling point.

"I want a bench made from a convent door," people insisted when they called or dropped by our shop. They were hot items.

The best part of our small business venture was that a few of our guys were becoming good carvers and artisans and they could customize nearly any design that was brought to them. Jose Gomez, a carver from Guadalajara, was the carving coach. Jose worked in both wood and stone. He had learned his craft in Mexico when he was young. His lean, strong hands were his instrument. Each of his fingers was the length of a banana and they were pared down to the essential bone and muscle that was needed to create a work of art.

As the business emerged, Dominic assumed the role of general manager, Jose Gomez was the artist and I hovered about them both as creative consultant. Of the first three hundred benches that we constructed, none left the property without my seal of approval. I loved the smell of the freshly cut wood. Birch, maple, oak, pine, teak—each wood had a unique history and was grown in a different forest. Here in our makeshift wood-shop their mingled aromas filled the air with expectation and purpose.

What we didn't know about woodwork, furniture construction, and running a business could have fit into the back of several pick-up trucks. We were high on imagination though, and somehow we convinced our first hundred customers that "pride of ownership" was linked to owning a Taller San Jose product.

A year and a half after we began selling benches, we ran into trouble. The problem was with the convent door benches. They were actually made of pieced-pine—panels made up of small pieces of wood that had been glued together. In an outdoor environment, the pieced-pine benches were doomed from the start. We had made our first *designer* bench for the bishop and we presented it to him on the occasion of his seventy-fifth birthday. The workers had carved his coat of arms on the back and it was a glorious piece of art. Some months later, the bishop called to report that his bench was having problems. He didn't tell us that the seat had fallen out. Unfortunately the bench had been sitting on top of a sprinkler where it was watered regularly, expanding the wood. Then the sun beat down on the damp wood all day and loosened the glued pine pieces until they were in shambles. We made the bishop a sturdier bench but then we had to stand ready for some other recalls on the convent door products.

Our inexperience, combined with the fact that our trainees weren't always regular, responsible employees, cut into what we expected to be a narrow profit margin. The truth is, we lost money. Still, the benefits outweighed the losses. We employed a number of unstable young men and kept them off the streets and out of jail. Some actually became good woodworkers surpassing their early instructors and we learned from our mistakes.

Before we had an enclosed truck, we used our pick-up to make deliveries, tying down the benches with strong cords and ropes. One afternoon I received an emergency call from big, strong Dominic. It was the only time I'd ever heard him shaken up. He'd been driving down the freeway at a good clip with a bench tied down in the back of the truck when he felt a sudden lunge. The bench, which weighed well over a hundred pounds, had catapulted skyward and then landed with a crash in between lanes of fast moving traffic. Cars and trucks screeched their brakes and diverted their paths to dodge the remnants of the bench and to avoid colliding with each other.

"Is it still sitting in the middle of the freeway?" I asked him.

"No," he said, "it's just a bunch of toothpicks." So much for a sacred convent door!

We had started the bench building business indoors but the noise from the table saws, the film of fine sawdust, and the stench of varnish forced us to negotiate with the city to obtain more out-door space. After months of pleading, they conceded and offered us a small empty building adjacent to our property. Over time we took squatters' rights and expanded into other nearby abandoned quarters. But the work environment was never satisfactory. There was no one space where all the young men could work at the same time and it was hard to supervise the nooks and crannies of the out buildings.

Three years into the furniture business, we had heavy rains that lasted late into the spring. Day after day water poured through the ceiling and onto the workers as if there was no roof at all. The building repairs were costly and the flood of water had warped our wood supply.

It was a messy business that we had gotten ourselves into—the buildings, our starter furniture products, and the workers themselves. From time to time one of our young workers would fail to show up for work just when we needed him most. He'd had a court appearance that he'd failed to mention or a meeting with his probation officer. Occasionally one of our most dependable young workers would simply disappear—he would be in jail.

By fits and starts, we learned the pitfalls of entrepreneurship and along the way we created some beautiful furniture—not just benches, but entertainment centers, credenzas, hope chests, and chapel furnishings. Finally, we were able to save for a bigger building. When we made the move to the new quarters, we were also able to expand the training program to incorporate the broader construction related trades of framing, drywall installa-tion, and roofing.

In spite of the ups and downs of our shaky business, we'd been able to train and employ a significant number of young men and keep them out of jail. If they fell into trouble, were arrested and jailed again, they had someplace to return to other than the mean streets that had corrupted them in the first place.

The wood business and the workers were in some strange ways analogous. The business was rocky, the production schedule uncertain, and the workers were as rough and unfinished as the raw wood they handled.

CHAPTER TEN

If you survive, your purpose will surface.

—Ken Correa

One morning Eddie Vargas didn't show up for his job at the bench business. His brother Omar, who also worked for us, told me that Eddie had been involved in a bar fight the previous evening and that he was now in jail. Eddie was one of our most reliable workers and I'd learned to count on him. He had been with us for over three years, first as a student and then as an employee. He'd worked alongside us for days during the messy building renovation, putting his muscles to work for the common good. Eddie was generous with his time, and whatever I asked of him, he did willingly. Best of all, even though he'd been deeply involved in a gang, in the three years that he had spent at Taller San Jose, he hadn't been caught up in any criminal activity. I saw him as an eager young worker, a husband, and a father—a success story—and he filled me with hope for other young men who were still buried in the gang.

When Omar first told me about his Eddie's arrest and incarceration, I was disappointed but not alarmed. There hadn't been a shooting or a stabbing, Omar said, and no one had been seriously injured. Whatever Eddie's involvement, I believed that he would soon be released.

I was wrong. I soon began to learn what deep, dark holes young men can dig for themselves when they first become involved in a gang, how a paper trail identifies them as a gang member forever, and how this gang designation can threaten to drag them downward no matter how hard they try to redeem themselves.

In the neighborhood in which he grew up, Eddie had learned to protect himself from the time he was nine or ten years old. Even as a preteen, when he left his apartment, he faced challenges from the older boys—those who controlled the territory and set the rules of the street. Eddie was jumped into the gang himself when he was fifteen years old. From that point on, his homies, his fellow gang members, dictated his behaviors and the game plan for protection and revenge.

When he turned eighteen, Eddie's gang was involved in a drive-by shooting. Although no one was killed or injured, all of the gang members were rounded up and arrested for attempted murder. Eddie, along with his fellow gang members, was indicted and charged with a felony. From that moment onward, Eddie's criminal record would weigh him down for the rest of his life. His police file now identified him as both a gang member and a felon. Eddie was incarcerated for several months. He was in jail when his first child was born.

When he was released, the local parish priest recommended that he check out Taller San Jose. Eddie was relieved to have a place to land where he could study and grow without defending himself on the streets all day and he was a serious and purposeful student. He had left school when he was fifteen and now he set the goal of finishing high school within a year's time. I would often see him sitting by himself in a remote corner of the building, creating a silent nest where he could study without distraction. His discipline and persistence paid off. At twenty, he graduated in cap and gown, with his wife and two young children at his side.

Eddie was a key figure in his extended family. He spoke English better than anyone else. He was better educated than the others and he was their protector. The family placed their hopes on him.

The Vargas family had come to California from Mexico when Eddie was four years old. Now he was an adult and he needed to work to support his young family and so he asked my help in finding an immigration attorney who could help him establish his legal residency. In order to achieve this status, he had to demonstrate proof that he had been a continuous resident in the United States for the past fifteen years and he had to get favorable reports from his probation officer to show that he had turned his life around. It was a time consuming and cumbersome process, complicated by the fact that Eddie was now a felon. I was annoyed that his parents had not done this legal work for him years ago when his life was not complicated by gang involvement and a criminal record.

"My parents tried to do this when I was a kid," Eddie answered my unasked question, "but they didn't have the money. It was going to cost them fifteen hundred dollars and they never had that money all at the same time. They just couldn't do it."

I had been to his family's apartment—where Eddie, his wife, children, parents, brothers, and sisters lived in crowded quarters. His parents didn't speak English. The stepfather took whatever kind of manual labor he could find to support the family. They were very poor. After my visit I stopped judging his parents for their negligence and got back to work helping Eddie achieve his goal of becoming a citizen.

When Eddie was arrested for the bar fight, his hopes and dreams for a promising future began to unravel. He'd had too much to drink. When the bar brawl broke out and someone attacked his friend, Eddie had picked up a beer bottle and hit the perpetrator over the head. He hadn't even known his name.

I went to visit Eddie in jail. I wanted to hear his side of the story and I wanted to let him know that whatever happened, God still cared about him and that I did too.

My stomach turns when I go to the jail. The visiting process is tedious, sterile. I feel like a prisoner myself. The rules are clear. Don't wear certain colors, the instructions read, and don't carry a bag or purse. Don't carry anything. Stand in this line; now that one. Wait. Just yourself and your ID. Take a seat and wait some more. Wait until they call your number. I was one number; Eddie was another. I found my way to the little visitor's booth and waited for him to show.

I'd grown to trust Eddie in the past three years. I'd known him as husband and father, an advocate for his younger brothers—watching over them, keeping them out of trouble. I'd known him as a leader in his family, the one who navigated the system for the Spanish speakers. He carried a lot on his shoulders for a young man of twenty-one.

I'd not known him as an *inmate*, anonymously dressed in a bright saffron jump suit. It robbed him of his dignity. We talked for awhile—on the phone—with a thick glass panel between us. I filled him in on the details of his defense. We talked about the money it would cost. I'd read the police report. I told him what I'd read. *Were there any witnesses who saw it differently?* The attorney wanted to know. Eddie didn't think that there were.

"I picked up the beer bottle and hit this guy on the head," he said. "He was beating on my friend. And then my friend took off and the police came and everybody pointed at me. That's what happened."

Eddie always told it as it was. He wasn't a blamer. He owned his sins.

And so Eddie was charged for assault with a deadly weapon. It was his second felony.

The police report emphasized the words *deadly weapon*. It was a beer bottle, for Christ's sake. How about a knife or a gun—I think about knives and guns when I hear the words *deadly weapon*. You buy or trade or steal to get a *deadly weapon*. You know the feel of it—the smooth, cold feel of the handle, how it molds to the grasp of your hand. When you are a person of violence and you own a *deadly weapon*, you know where it is and you remember to bring it with you when you leave the house. And if you happen to forget, just before you close the door, your violent inner voice kicks in, *Oh, I forgot my gun,* it says. *I've got to get my gun.* You hide it under your long, baggy shirt. You count on that *deadly weapon* because you're headed down a path of near certain violence and where you're going other people have *deadly weapons* too.

But Eddie hadn't brought a knife or gun with him that night in the bar. He'd hit someone he didn't even know with a beer bottle that had been close at hand. The criminal justice system didn't make distinctions. The bottle was a deadly weapon and Eddie was already a felon. What was one more heavy black mark on his already sullied brown record?

When our visiting time was up, Eddie turned to go and he waved to me as the heavy, steel door closed hard behind him. I started to cry. In his young life, he had created the hideous paper trail of a double felon. His wretched early history would follow him forever. But that's not how I knew Eddie. I'd tutored him in geometry and celebrated with him when he graduated from high school. I'd asked favors of him and he of me. I trusted Eddie, the felon, with my life.

❧

Young men like Eddie, who grow up in neighborhoods surrounded by racial segregation and indigence, walk though a subtle but hazardous minefield as they attempt to make their way into the adult world. Where they live, there are few, if any, models for what it means to be a productive provider. They may have been told that the world is filled with opportunity and promise but they haven't seen it and there is no one to show them the route to success. But the gang is out there ahead of them and the gang purports to understand the individual's hopelessness and pain far better than any family member or educational professional could, and so they make their moves on the younger vulnerable prey. Seasoned gang members put a critical question to emerging teens when they come out of their apartment doors.

"Where are you from?" they challenge.

It's not an innocent question meant to invite polite conversation but rather a test of loyalty and affiliation. The wrong answer can mean death—or at least a brutal pounding.

Whose side are you on, who do you hang with, what's your gang, are you with us or with our enemies?

To survive, many young men feel compelled to align themselves with the strongest pack in the neighborhood. One way to avoid this bullying pressure is to be identified as a *schoolie*. Schoolies are those who are successful in the academic world and local gang members view them as weak and powerless—sissies. Schoolies are useless to the gang and so they are left alone. But when you are young and vulnerable, it doesn't feel like a choice at all. You do what you have to do in order to survive.

CHAPTER ELEVEN

As I lay down in my bed, I think and I ask myself, "Will I live to see one more day or should this be my last day?"
— Israel Ramirez

I gave Luis Peralta a key to my heart the first day that we met. Luis was not the brightest young man or the best. When first I met him, he was a gang member. At eighteen, he had spent six months in jail for aggravated assault—a gang-related crime. In his gang, the "Crazy Perverted Criminals," his code name was "Sonic." He never told me that, but I saw it on a police report.

Luis didn't know it, but he had a hold on me before I even saw his face. He called Taller San Jose at the urging of his probation officer and I saw his name on a phone memo. His name was familiar to me in a nostalgic sort of way and the sound of it filled me with wonder and curiosity. There was a Luis Peralta far back in my own family history—a distant relative on my father's side of the family. The Luis Peralta that I knew was a leather jacket soldier who had come across the Sonoran desert into California in 1776 with the Anza expedition. He came from Mexico even before there was a Mexico.

And so I had prayed for the modern day Luis Peralta before I ever met him. I wondered who he was, why he had called, if he would actually walk in the door and if his roots were in any way connected to my own. I must have welcomed Luis warmly when we first met because in some remote way I had already identified him as a *primo*—a distant cousin from the past. We bonded quickly, as if we mattered to one another. I learned over time that, indeed, he was born in a rural village near where my ancestors had lived for generations—Valle San Luis, in Northern Sonora,

Mexico. Luis came with his mother to California when he was a year old. His brother was in prison here in California, his father was in prison in Mexico.

Luis was a boxer. I guess he had punched someone out in anger a time or two because the police had designated his fists as "lethal weapons," meaning that if he used them in violence, he could be indicted for a felony. Luis dressed like a gang member. His oversized pant legs formed pools of worn fringe where his feet were supposed to emerge. A gigantic shirt diminished his powerful frame. His hair was clipped one stop short of bald.

You're not going to make it in Orange County looking like that! I thought. I knew better than to share my thoughts aloud. Luis thought he looked just fine. He had joined the club years before. His clothes signaled his belonging. He didn't know any other way to look.

The gang, to me, seems a perverse form of scouting. It recruits young boys from the neighborhood, instills values, creates bonds, and offers rewards. By the time a boy is sixteen or seventeen, he can earn the equivalent of Eagle Scout status. But the system is twisted and evil. The neophytes are pawns of a Mafia-like system. They are used to create and grow a drug market. They are senselessly and violently pitted against each other. It is all about money, greed, and power. The values held up to youth are perverse, the bonds deceptive, the rewards transitory. And the stakes are high. You can be maimed for life. You can die.

There hadn't been any men in Luis's home for a long time. The gang had let him in and provided him with the only model he knew of what it meant to be a man.

I read one time that in nature there are certain insects that, along with their poisonous venom, also inject an anesthetic so that the prey becomes numb and doesn't notice what is happening. Inculcation into the gang must be like that. The young person doesn't get the whole picture until it's too late. Then they're trapped. Was that how it was for Luis? Had he made a choice or had he been unwittingly trapped?

~❦~

Luis had a hard time hanging on at Taller, but he almost always showed up for his computer class. I felt protective of him. I was convinced that he was a distant cousin, so while I tried to treat him objectively, my heart was warm toward him—I considered him blood. He was under house arrest of sorts related to his probation and he had a woman, Frieda. Luis stayed home all day and took care of Frieda's son while she was working. He didn't have right-to-work documents. He couldn't work legitimately, but before his time in jail he'd found work on the side, in construction, when he could. If he was found on the street or hanging around his old friends, he could be arrested and jailed again for violating his probation. So Luis was either at home as a childcare provider or at Taller San Jose. A dull life for an eighteen year old kid! I wanted him to do well but I couldn't make it happen. He had to do that himself.

Not long after I had met him, I invited Luis to accompany me to the Orange County Register award luncheon. He hemmed and hawed but finally said yes. I told him he'd have to get some new clothes—"grown-up clothes," I called them. He scowled. We made a date to go shopping together. I didn't know anything about guy clothes and I knew that I was going to be asking him to stretch his sense of style—considerably. His new clothes needed to be just one notch up from "gang-land," otherwise they'd scare him off. We ended up at Macy's. When we got to the men's' department, I found some young guy to help us. There was no way Luis was going to take any direction from me about what looked good and what didn't. I backed up—backed way up—but it wasn't easy. He ended up with a pair of khaki pants and a banded collared shirt— one that could be tucked in. I thought he looked really sharp. I used my birthday money to make the purchase. Men's clothes look so simple and cost so much! On the way home, Luis told me that the only other time he was in Macy's, he'd stolen the clothes.

"How did you do it?" I asked.

"Just put on extra stuff in the dressing room," he said. "I feel bad now. I used to do that kinda stuff all the time."

Luis was supposed to meet me at Taller the next day so that we could drive to the award luncheon together. He called me and told me he couldn't do it.

"Why," I asked. "What's going on?"

"I can't get there. I can't be on the streets with these kinda clothes. People'll see me. I don't look right."

"Come on, Luis," I chided. "You only live eight blocks away."

"Can't do it. Can't be seen," he responded. He explained to me again the impossible awkwardness of walking down the street in somebody else's clothes.

I picked him up.

We won an award that day. It was Taller San Jose's first public award. It was a big deal. Luis and I were both excited and I could tell he liked being part of the whole thing. After that, we were thick, Luis and I, though he still didn't believe we were *primos*.

The day after the award luncheon the shirt and pants were neatly folded and sitting on my desk. There was a note attached. "You can have them back," it said. I called him to ask what had happened.

"I don't want the f ——in' clothes," he said. His voice was low, hurt-like.

He'd been late for class that day. One of the instructors had scolded him. She'd told him he wasn't getting anything out of the program except for his fancy new clothes, that Taller had paid for his fancy new clothes. He'd been dissed.

I was mad, too. I was so new at my relationships with the street kids that I was sometimes uncertain about when I crossed a line. When was I coddling, when was I challenging. I wasn't sure, but I knew that getting him the clothes was not a capital sin.

"Listen, Luis," I told him. "That wasn't Taller's money. That was my money. I can do whatever I want with it. You did me a favor by coming with me. I wanted to get you the new duds. It's that simple."

He came and picked up his clothes the next day. I didn't see him for awhile after that. He stopped coming to class.

⊱⊰

When he did return it was to ask my help with his immigration papers. He met all the criteria for becoming a legal resident. He had been in the country continuously for the past nineteen years, since he was an infant. Although he had previously filed all the legal paperwork through an immigration attorney, it was a three year wait for the processing to be completed. I learned that this was not an uncommon phenomenon—the long wait. The INS was overwhelmed with such requests and was under no particular pressure to act on the applications. It was critical for Luis, though. He couldn't work without documentation of his legal status. His mother, the breadwinner in the family, had a bad heart. She did factory work at night. He wanted to help her financially. He felt that he was rotting away at home. This was a dilemma that I'd met among former gang members; they were trying to get out of the gang and the old neighborhood to move ahead in life. A full-time job offers the most hope. But if they're sitting on the immigration border, they are stuck. It's not a good thing to have young, healthy, energetic former gang members hanging around all day with nothing to do. It spells big trouble.

I helped Luis draft a letter to his immigration attorney asking for an update on his status and to his probation officer asking for a positive recommendation regarding his behavior.

When he left my office he gave me a big hug. We'd become *primos*, I thought. Did he think so, too? At least he knew that I cared about him very much.

A month or so later I looked up from my desk to see a gray-faced Luis before me. He'd slipped into my office without my noticing.

"What's wrong?" I asked.

"Frieda left." I'd never seen him so distressed. I'd seen his angry face, his worried face, but not this very sad one.

"Luis, what happened?" I persisted.

He shrugged. He looked as if he were about to cry.

We sat down together in my office. He was silent for awhile and then began to pour out his grief. She'd grown restless. She wanted more from him. People had told her she could do better. He didn't know what more he could do.

Even though I'd come to love Luis, I thought that at times he had an inflated opinion of himself and what he brought to a relationship.

"Well, *Precisoso,* look at it objectively," I pushed a little. "You haven't finished your diploma. You don't have any money. You don't have a job. You've been in trouble and you've spent nine months in prison. You don't sound like a prince to me."

He looked up at me helplessly. His wry smile briefly acknowledged the reality of my assessment. Then he grew quite sad again.

"I miss Ritchie, too," said Luis. Ritchie was Frieda's five-year old son. Luis had spent nearly every day of the past three years with him while Frieda was working. He had developed a father's tender heart. When he began to talk about Ritchie, he started to tear up.

How tough these kids look on the outside, I thought. *Most people would cross the street if they were alone and saw them coming, but they're soft inside. They love. They fear. They're scared. They're vulnerable.*

I couldn't take away Luis's pain, but he allowed me to pray with him. I made the sign of the cross on his forehead and told him that God would be with him in his darkest days. I urged him to keep in touch.

I'd never been around young men when they'd lost their loves and were grieving from rejection. It was the first time, but not the last, that I accepted the tears of a tough, young man.

≈⊱✦⊰≈

Several months later when I walked into the front office, Letty Zamora, our office manager motioned me aside. She pointed out a pretty young woman who was sitting on one of our benches in the lobby. She couldn't have been more than sixteen and she was visibly pregnant.

"Do you see that girl?" Letty nodded toward her. "She's carrying Luis's baby."

I knew not to question Letty's information. She worked the front office like a sweet and savvy undercover cop. She knew everything and she was always accurate about her facts.

I felt sick inside. Luis had never talked to me about this girl. If this was true, and I was certain that it was, I felt nothing but anger and contempt for Luis. He had used her.

The next time I saw him, he admitted it. He had been lonely. It was easy sex. He didn't care a thing about her. He had no intention of standing by her in any real sense.

I scolded him, reminding him of what it was like for him to grow up without a father who was present and cared about him. "Forget it," I said. "You don't know what it was like not to have a loving father. You only know that it happened to you. If you really knew the pain it can cause, you wouldn't have used that girl for your quick and easy pleasure." I was mad and deeply disappointed in him.

He acted appropriately chastised. His pale Mexican skin turned red and he looked down. I thought about the girl a lot after that. He barely knew her name.

꘎꘎꘎

Luis told me when the baby was born and announced in a sheepish manner that he was now a father.

"Were you with Maria when the baby came?" I asked.

"No," he responded. "She didn't want me around and neither did her family."

That wasn't hard to understand.

He seemed awkward and contrite about the whole affair. I didn't say much. I'd already given him "the complete scolding."

"Listen, *Precioso*," I said, "just don't go having any more babies without talking with me first. You hurt that girl and that baby needs a father."

꘎꘎꘎

By Christmas Luis and Frieda were back together and Frieda was pregnant. Luis was ecstatic and excited about being a father again. I had mixed feelings. I found it hard to share his enthusiasm. I was still thinking about the first baby who was not even a year old. Who was father to him? But who was I in this relationship anyway—a fairy godmother? A distant cousin from another time and place? I thought and felt like a mom.

A month before the new baby was to be born, Frieda, Luis's girlfriend, called me. Luis was in jail, she told me and he would be there for several weeks. He was arrested for aggravated assault. His sister had called him the night before. She had been having a fight with her husband and it had turned violent. She wanted to get her little daughters out of the house and she'd asked Luis to come and get them. Luis had just been released from the hospital following surgery for a double hernia and he was still in pain. He didn't think he could get the girls on his own and invited a friend to come with him. He'd made a poor choice; the friend had a gun.

Frieda told me that things had gotten ugly between Luis and his brother-in-law. They got into a verbal shouting match and threats were made. The brother-in-law threatened to call the police and Luis and his friend left the scene—fast. Luis's friend had dropped his gun when he ran down the stairs. The police came and later picked up both Luis and his friend. No one had been injured; but Luis, because he was a former gang member, faced serious charges—eight years in prison.

A few days I later I found a soft puffy envelope in my mailbox. Luis had sent it from jail. He had enclosed a pencil drawing of St. Joseph—the logo for Taller San Jose, on a white cloth napkin.

The letter read:

Hi Prima,

How are you? I hope and pray for all of us God's children to be OK. As 4 me I'm OK but I could be better if I was out a free man. First of all I want you to know that I'm kicking my self for being in this situation but I also know that God works in misterios ways and this probably happened for a good reason. I do believe that it is for me to see my life as a new person in other words to think twice not once. I just hope God can give me a chance. I do have a baby on the way and I have been doing a lot of praying because I do want to be there for my baby when he comes into this world.

Thanks a lot 4 your support. Prima—tell everyone that I love them. I miss visiting you.

Love, Luis Peralta

P.S. Be happy.

When Luis was out on bail, we talked about the charges that he was facing and the fact that the police had noted the incident as gang related, a designation that can double the sentence. Luis was facing a hearing at which he either had to accept a felony with a possible sixteen months in jail or go to trial. He swore that he did not have a gun the evening of the altercation with his brother-in-law and that his fingerprints could not be found on a gun. I believed him. Luis was now caught between pleading guilty to a felony and jeopardizing his immigration status or facing a trial with an uncertain outcome. If he was found guilty, he could spend eight years in prison.

"I didn't do nothin'," Luis told me. "I can't do eight years in prison. I won't be the same after. I'll have to act different in there—have to protect myself. I can get in trouble in there even if I don't want to. I've changed inside. Doing time will change me back to my old self. I'm different inside now, not like I was before. I don't wanna go back to that bad place inside me. I didn't do nothin'," he said again.

"Didn't do *anything*," I suggested.

"That's what I said, I didn't do nothin'."

"Listen," I said, "When you say, 'I didn't do nothin',' you sound *maleducado*. Try saying, 'I didn't do *anything*.' It'll sound better if you're in court. Say it a hundred times a day. Look in the mirror and say it while you're brushing your teeth."

I wrote it down for him while at the same time giving him my grammar lesson on the importance of double negatives in Spanish and their forbidden use in English. The emphasis on grammar didn't seem important just then, but I wanted him to sound right. I thought it might give him an edge.

He folded my grammar paper in half and shoved it in his pocket.

"Do you want to pray?" I asked. He nodded. His eyes teared up.

I pulled out the prayer that John Henry Cardinal Newman had written over a hundred years ago when he was down and out. I didn't give Luis a history lesson about Newman. I just told him that Newman was a good guy who a lot of people treated poorly. I told Luis that no matter who was against him, that God knew his heart—that to God, and to his mother and to his girlfriend, Frieda, and to me, he was *precioso*. Nobody could take that from him.

I read Newman's words slowly.

God has created me to do him some definite service.
He has committed some work to me that he has not committed to
another...
Therefore I will trust Him.
Whatever I am, I can never be thrown away.
If I am in sickness, my sickness may serve Him.
If I am in sorrow, my sorrow may serve Him.
He does nothing in vain.
He knows what He is about.
He may take away my friends.
He may throw me among strangers.
He may make me feel desolate,
Make my spirits sink,
Hide my future from me—still He knows what He is about.[2]

I skipped the phrase, *I shall be an angel of peace, a preacher of truth;* that was a bit of a stretch for Luis. When I finished, he took the prayer, too, folded it, and put it in his pocket.

Afterward, I let him read the letter that I had sent to his attorney—reiterating what I knew about Luis, how long ago he had left gang life behind, how I viewed the situation as I understood it—a family squabble, not a gang related crime. I emphasized without passion or naiveté how young people of color were treated differently than the rest of us, how once the cards were stacked against them, they could be labeled for life. What I didn't say, but firmly believed, was that if Luis were the son of a successful attorney, physician, or CEO in another part of the county, he wouldn't be facing the same charges.

Luis asked me if I would call the district attorney assigned to his case and tell her what I had told the defense attorney.

"I don't know if it'll do any good, Luis. It's about winning and losing for attorneys. I don't know if she'll even talk to me."

"Talk to her," he pleaded. "You're white," he said, pointing to my skin. "You talk white. She'll listen to you. *Do* it, Sister Eileen."

In the front office, he called his girlfriend, Frieda, and got the name of the district attorney assigned to his case. He handed it to me. "Call her," he pleaded again. "Talk white to her."

"I'll call the Deputy Public Defender," I pledged, "and ask his advice."

As Luis got ready to leave, his eyes were sad and pleading.

"I didn't do nothin'," I said, doing my best to imitate his inflection.

"Didn't do *anything*," he echoed back.

❧❦❧

Luis, anguished, and on the advice of his attorney, settled for a plea bargain—a felony with a reduced sentence. He was now twenty-five years old with two small sons that he was trying to support. Things went hard for him in the sentencing phase because he'd had a prior offense when he was eighteen—when he was running with the gang. Once you have a gang affiliation you don't shake it off with your fellow homies, your rivals, or the police. No matter how much you try to change your life and behavior, the past reaches out to pull you down—to remind you of your lowest moments, to rub your face in your own dirt.

Luis spent eleven months in the state prison at Wasco. His letters told me that it was tough. Just before Luis was sentenced there, an eighteen-year-old youth had been killed by his cellmate. The whole prison was on lock-down—that meant that inmates were confined to their cells for all but one hour of the day—for weeks. Wasco was no frills—no educational opportunities, no recreation, no work assignments, and no church services. I wrote to Luis encouraging him to keep a low profile, to try to stay out of trouble. I didn't know how to phrase my words—what did I know about being young, male, Hispanic, and in prison?

He was taken to the Mexican border by bus when he was released—no money and no clothes—except those on his back. He hadn't been to Mexico since he was an infant and Frieda and his sons were in California. A week later he called me. He was in Santa Ana. He didn't want me to see him.

"I lost thirty pounds in prison," he said, "and most of my hair fell out. I look real ugly."

He came the next day.

"What are you going to do now?" I asked. It made me sad to see him so scrawny, sallow, and jumpy. It wasn't the Luis I'd known before.

"I'll find work," he said, and he did.

❧

"I didn't ever really have a father," Luis told me one day. He had his two little sons with him and he was beaming. "These kids are going to have a dad," he said. He was good with kids. He'd helped to raise Frieda's son. Parenting brought out a soft and joyous side of him.

Luis was doing construction but having trouble finding steady work. He wanted to keep the money flowing in, wanted to make up for the time he'd spent in prison.

Several weeks later Frieda called to tell me that Luis had been shot twice and that he was in the hospital. Her brother was wounded too, and he was in worse shape than Luis. They'd been at a *quinciñiera*—a traditional Mexican party to celebrate the coming of age of a fifteen-year-old girl. A past rival had recognized Frieda's brother as he was leaving the rented hall. Frieda said that she and Luis and the children had been standing right next to her brother.

Luis was shot through the chest and in the hand with .45 magnum revolver. One bullet had narrowly missed his heart. It had ripped through his lung instead.

I visited him in the hospital. His lung was going to heal. It pained him to breathe because the bullet had also shattered some of his ribs. His hand was wrapped in a swath of bandages. He kept it elevated. I wondered what the hand looked like inside its gauze cocoon.

"Can you loan me some money?" he asked humbly. "I can't work for awhile. I'll need some medicine."

"Sure," I said, but I knew that it wouldn't be a loan and I knew that the resources that I could muster wouldn't touch the cost of his recuperation.

I felt strangely quiet inside when I'd first heard that Luis had been shot. A sense of fatalistic inevitability iced my veins. I didn't want to feel anything. I wanted to distance myself—to leave the scene, to pretend that it had happened to someone else, someone I didn't know.

Is this what happens to the kids involved in gangs? I wondered. *Do they become inured to the outrage of injury and death? Is it the deadening of sensibility that allows them to kill and to put their own lives at risk?* I wanted to push Luis away. I didn't want to have to grieve for him if he might someday die a violent death.

But it was too late. I already cared for Luis. I already loved him.

"You don't care for someone—give him or her a home, some food, your time—in order that she or he gets better, or things turn out right," states Mary Lou Kownacki, OSB, a Benedictine nun and poet, who has spent years running a homeless shelter. *"You care for someone because you care for someone. You love someone because you love someone."*[3]

When Luis was out of the hospital he called me. "I don't want to bother you," he said, "but I hurt so bad that I have to talk to somebody. Is it okay?"

I was glad to hear from him. He was quick to tell me what was going on in his mind and heart.

"I want to die," he said. "My hand is bad—real bad. It's gone. I can't use it for nothing. It's useless—like a big purple fish hangin' off the end of my arm. I just came back from the doctor and they showed me the x-rays. There's no bones in there, man—just splinters and mush. I want to kill that guy who shot me. I want to hurt him as bad as he hurt me. I don't want to live like this."

"I'm sorry, Luis." I didn't know what to say. I knew enough not to give him a pious lecture, but I couldn't imagine what words could comfort him. I listened.

"I have a broken bone in my thumb," he went on, "but my fingers are gone. They're gonna try to take some bone from my butt or somethin and make some new bones in my hand."

The boxer in him was finished. I pictured his long, painful, and incomplete recuperation.

"I'll never be the same," he cried.

I was certain that he wouldn't.

"I want to kill that guy," he repeated. The mentality of the gang visited its fury upon him.

"I know you want to kill him, Luis, but you can't do it now cause you're too weak. It's natural to feel revenge. I think I'd want to kill him too. That's part of being human."

"Why did God let this happen?" he sobbed. "You know I haven't done nothing wrong for a long time. I've been goin' to church. I read the Bible. Why did this happen, Sister Eileen?"

I didn't know. "I'm sorry," I repeated.

"What am I gonna do?" he asked.

"You're going to take one day at a time, Luis. And you're going to ask God to help you." I wanted to talk to him about the power that hate would have to embitter him, to turn its evil upon him, to turn him evil—he the victim, the wounded. Just now, however, he didn't need my preaching; he just wanted me to care.

I told him how I carried him in my heart each day. The shooting had thrust him back into the circle of gang violence, vengeance, and payback. If he could walk away from it once again, it was going to be through conversion of heart and the power of prayer. Nothing else had the power to heal such raw and brutal pain. I could only comfort him for the moment. It was God who would have to do the healing.

Anger and wrath, these also are abominations, yet a sinner holds on to them, says the Book of Sirach (Sir 27:30). I know. I've clung to wrath and anger. I've been humbled by the power of its obsession. I know how slow I've been to release my wrath—even while praying for the grace to do so. But I'd never been shot. I'd not had my body rearranged forever by a .45 magnum bullet.

❈

When I think of those who are oppressed and in bondage, I remember the woeful mournings of God's chosen people in captivity. And then I am reminded of the young men in the yellow prison jumpsuits who appear one after the other behind the cages in the courtrooms each day. It is almost impossible for me to look at them. Most are not old enough or jaded enough to be real criminals. They need a way out of poverty and gangs and crime.

I've been reading Henri Nouwen's book, *The Return of the Prodigal Son.*[4] It talks about our uneven self-concept and how our woundedness can sometimes catch us unawares. In *The Return of the Prodigal Son,* Nouwen gives a dramatic image of God the Father's all-embracing love for each of us—for me. Using the parable of the wayward young man and his loving father, he describes a God who actively goes out looking for me, whose face lights up when He sees me, who wants to give me all that is His, who would throw a big party just for me.

Like most other human beings, however, I can't really grasp this. When I do believe it, I can't hold the consolation in my mind or heart for long. Over my lifetime, I've learned through my parents, teachers, and the competition of life that in some ways I am flawed—not quite good enough. In spite of an enormous amount of education, numerous accomplishments in my life and significant affirmation, down deep a part of me believes that I don't quite measure up to the expectations of the world.

It's that little wounded piece of me that gets pierced again when I am dissed, when someone doesn't recognize how precious I am and doesn't treat me accordingly. When my pride is offended, there's not much that can soothe me, because down deep a part of me buys into the fact that I'm not worthy. I just don't want to be reminded of that fact!

I'm old enough to rant and rave and let time heal my wounds. If there's someone around who can help me process my rage and won't add to my fury by his own blind-sidedness, it helps for me to vent. Ultimately, it is good to have friends and family who let me know that I'm loved even when I mess up.

As I deal with my own experience of being dissed and process my woundedness, I am challenged as to how to help Luis and his friends deal with the insecurities and angers that paralyze them and get them into so much trouble—sometimes into jail. The first thing is to let them know that they are deeply loved and to show them in some concrete and earthly way the unconditional love of a God they may not yet know. But I also want to find a way to share with them that I, too, understand dissed and its power. I want to honor their rage and learn with them about how to move on.

CHAPTER TWELVE

Without anyone's help, I fought for that little person inside of me. I was alone and pregnant with nobody but my bed and my memories. I hope that my little boy becomes a good man and has the guts to face the world like his mamma did.

—Norma Aguilar

The stakes are high for young unsupervised preadolescents—especially for those whose parents work two and three jobs just to provide rent and food. In the barrio neighborhoods, the hours between the dark and the daylight are the times when drugs are bought and sold, when babies are hastily conceived, and when the guns come out. It's hard to find the path back to childhood once it's been bartered for trouble.

Where were their parents? I wondered when I first learned how early the young people in my neighborhood dropped out of school, got pregnant, or were assigned to detention centers. *What part had the churches or schools played in their lives?*

When these young people first started to stray, did no one chase after them, grab them by the shoulders, look them in the eye and say, "I love you precious child. You are flesh of my flesh and bone of my bone. You are my most precious possession. I will watch over your every step until I know that you are safe and grown."

❧

Gustavo Torres described his quick downward spiral for me, painting the sad story in brisk verbal strokes. His parents' marriage had fallen apart when he was thirteen. He described how both his mom and his dad had retreated to their own painful corners, taking their eyes off their children—seeming to abandon them.

"They didn't care about me," he said, "so I didn't care about me. First I started to drink and then I turned to drugs. I used them and then I sold them."

Within a year, Gustavo was in juvenile hall. In that same year, he impregnated his girlfriend—though he knew little about her but her name.

⟞✴⟝

Antonio and Arturo, the Burgoa brothers, were just kids when their troubles started. Tony was born in Mexico and Art in California. Their mother left them with her family in Puebla while she tried to make a living north of the border. She visited them from time to time so that they would not forget her and when they were preteens, she brought them to Santa Ana. Neither Tony nor Art spoke English and school was a humiliating experience. Every day bullies taunted them on their way home, beating them up and promising more violence to come. Tony, the older by a year, determined to protect himself and his brother and so he drew a group of homeboys around him and they pledged honor to each other and loyalty before death. With little reflection or intention, they created their own gang. Before they were eighteen, one of their homies had been shot and killed, another wounded, and both of the Burgoas had landed in jail. Their mother, Mariacruz, was frantic with worry.

Mariacruz had raised her boys on her own while working twelve hours a day cleaning houses. In her off hours, she cared for her sons and caught some sleep. In spite of her grueling schedule, she barely managed to pay the rent and to put food on the table. When school was over each day and Tony and Art merged onto the streets, their mother was miles away earning their keep and there was no one to protect them.

In the forest, the mother bear weans her cubs in a time honored manner. When the cubs are nearing independence, she wanders off from them a little farther each day—first just a short ways off where she can keep an eye on them and later within earshot so that she might respond if they are in danger. She joins them at nightfall, checking on their safety and their progress. And then one day she wanders off for good. It's how her mother weaned her and taught her to survive.

But today, in Latino first- and second-generation immigrant families, the time honored cultural norms of the past are disrupted and the roles between parents and children are reversed. The kids get way out in front and their parents can no longer find them. The children most often speak English long before their parents. It is often the child who is the translator at school, at the medical clinic, in the bank, and with the landlord. In the barrio, when children enter their teens and the generation gap widens, many young Latinos intuit that their parents don't hold the map for the new terrain. They search for the path on their own—trusting neither their parents nor the institutions meant to support them. Instead, they look to their peers for direction.

"Can you imagine what I put my mother through?" asked Angie Morales. Angie is out of the gang life now, but she says that she spent at decade as a bad ass.

"Please be careful. Stay in the neighborhood. Don't drink too much. Don't come home too late, my mother would nag and yell at me."

"She didn't say these words just to bug me," says Angie. "She said them because she worried about me and because I was acting like a stupid kid—going out at night to the streets to show the world how down I was."

For poor Latino youth, navigating their way through crime-filled barrios is akin to maneuvering their course through a treacherous mine field. The traps are drugs, gangs, crime, early

sexual encounters with accompanying diseases, unplanned preg-
nancies, and violence of every kind. It's not for the timid.

❦

Lucia Beltran, a young woman in her twenties, is struggling
to stay ahead of her children. Her two boys, Ignacio and Xavier,
are eight and nine years old and she worries about them every
day. Recently she quit a good job because she was afraid for her
boys' safety. Ignacio, who has trouble in school, has already been
held back twice. His teacher, offering no solutions to his reading
problem, warned Lucia that he was on a path to criminal behavior. Lucia knows the scene. She knows the rules of the neighborhood and that her boys are ripe for early involvement in the gang
if she is not there every moment of every day to watch over them.

There are few role models for children in the barrios. While
several adults in each household work to pay the bills, few have
dignified work or steady work or work that pays beyond minimum wage. Whenever a family stabilizes and advances financially, they move away to better their own conditions and to keep
their children safe. A family poorer still replaces them and so the
barrio perpetuates itself and its poverty.

While parents do the best they can to keep their children in
school, when their backs are turned, often when they're at work,
the children have their own way. They make as if they're going to
class each day, but if they don't like school and there is no one to
notice, they stay home or hang out in local parks. Many of the
families in Santa Ana come from rural Mexico where there is less
educational opportunity than in the cities. If the parents only
went to the third grade or perhaps the sixth, they are not always
alarmed that their sons or daughters leave school at the age of fifteen. After all, these young people speak English and they've had
more schooling than anyone else in the family. If they are reluctant learners and have to be forced to go to class, they might as
well join the workforce and help the family to provide for itself.

Yet when young people fall out of school, they don't always find work. Instead, they stall like sailing ships becalmed on quiet seas. Frozen and fearful, they await a benevolent force to propel them forward or a magical power to proffer gainful employment. The guys are afraid to step ahead into their father's deep foot-prints. Their first generation immigrant fathers are the janitors, the gardeners, and the dishwashers—the minimum wage grunt workers of Southern California. The young men have seen their fathers get stuck at the bottom of the labor pool. They witness the frustration of the older generation first-hand and they see how alcohol is used to cover depression and how rage is acted out in violence. The young resist turning their own bodies into instru-ments of unskilled labor. But because they have no skills to offer and no work experience at all, they often do nothing but hang out with their friends where gang life, drugs, and crime lurk around the corners. In their languor, the young men with their baggy clothing, shaved heads, and tattoos signal to the world that they're not ready for any serious undertaking.

The girls have even fewer role models for education and employment. Most of their mothers are monolingual Spanish speakers who've spent their lives rearing children and doing low end factory work. What the girls do know is how to care for chil-dren. Many have been looking after their siblings since the age of six. Growing up in large families with their parents involved in endless labor, many of the girls, like their brothers, attach little meaning to their lives and hold out little hope for their futures.

But boys have the power to make girls feel special and wanted—even desirable. The guys, who appear to them to be more sexually experienced, flatter them and woo them and use them for their exploits. The shame of early pregnancy is painful but transitory. Once they become mothers, they have an age old pattern to follow. They're bodies tell them what to do next and when the baby comes, they know the drill. They now have an identity. They're moms.

Marisol Duran became a mom when she was fourteen years old. At twenty-three, she was a single mother with four boys. The oldest was nine.

Her landlord had told her about Taller San Jose. He'd heard about it in church and he thought it might help her. Marisol was on welfare and lived in a tiny duplex with her sons. The father of the boys, whom she had never married, was in and out of prison. He had nothing to offer them and she didn't count on him anymore for anything—for money, for shared parenting, for emotional support, or for affection. Marisol was trying to go back to school and she was scared. She'd dropped out of school when she was thirteen and pregnant and never had a chance to return. Now her three older boys were in school themselves and because she just had the toddler, Raul, to care for during the day, she had more free time. The boys were on a year round school schedule though and so when it came time for their month off—which was four times a year, Marisol had to stop whatever she was doing—school or work—and stay home with them. They were really pretty good kids and she managed them well. But they were boys, and they were all over each other if she wasn't in their midst. By the grace of God, Marisol was quite a good mother. She knew her role in the family. Not surprisingly, she had become old before her time. I tried to remember how I was at twenty-three, what I was doing, what my responsibilities were, how I felt inside. I was beginning to mature at that age, but there was no way in heaven that I could have managed as a single mother of four boys—full-time, non-stop, forever.

When Marisol had to stay home, I went over to tutor her and I asked one of the other sisters to do the same. I didn't want Marisol to lose track and give up her studies. She was eager to learn, but it was hard; there were so many distractions for her. I always called before I dropped by and I knew when I arrived that she had cleaned the place spotless—the best she could do with all the grubby handprints coming right after her to muck it up again. But I could tell she wanted me to see her at her best. It was easy to love Marisol.

Marisol was the center and strength of a sad and complex family. Her mother, her brother, and her sisters all looked to her as the family matriarch, as the one who could shoulder the family problems.

She stopped coming to class in the middle of the second semester and I called to find out what had happened. She sounded depressed; her voice was soft and low.

"I've got my brother's baby," she said. "I won't be able to come for awhile."

"Why are you caring for your brother's baby?" I asked. "Where is he? Where is the mother?"

She told me that the mother had had the baby in jail and that her brother didn't have any way to care for it.

I had some extra food that day—two boxes of donuts and a pizza. I drove them over to Marisol's. The baby girl was two days old. Marisol held her at arm's length. She didn't cuddle her. It was as if she'd had enough of mothering and there was nothing more within her to give to this sad, vulnerable infant. She was disgusted by her brother and his druggie girlfriend. They hadn't even given the baby a name. Marisol felt punished by their actions—and stuck. The girlfriend was going to be in jail for months. I spent some time with Marisol, letting her know that I loved her and that I cared, trying to find out how I could help her during this time.

When we finished visiting, I got into the car and started home but I soon had to pull over. I cried for Marisol, for the tiny nameless baby, and for all the poverty that I couldn't cure.

⚜

I've often dreamt about nursing fragile babies back to life. I wonder—is this an archetypal dream; do all women have it? Surely men don't dream about nursing babies; it must be a woman thing. But I wonder if women who have born children still dream of babies? Maybe childbirth and child rearing have been such a large part of their daily experience that there is no need for babies to visit them at night. I imagine that women who are infertile dream these dreams, those women whom the Scriptures referred to as barren. But I wonder, do other nuns dream about babies like I do? I should ask them.

The story lines that surround my dreams differ. They are wildly inventive, vividly particular in detail. Last night, in my dream world, I was handed a baby whose parents had been using drugs. The baby was three or four months old, shrunken, jaundiced, and weak. I was in the midst of a crowded room, but everyone who saw the baby ignored him or just walked away. My task is always clear—take the baby into my arms, cuddle him, warm him, nurse him from my breast, soothe him, and restore him to fullness of life. The vulnerable infant demands all the energy and attention that I can muster. It is a moment of crisis. It is a time for clear thinking and prompt action and yet I am not frantic, never anxious. The baby always lives—thrives.

Is the dream for me or for another? I've never felt that my maternal instincts were particularly strong or that I would have made a great mother. I wasn't around babies when I was young and, though at times I've longed for the intimacy of marriage and for the satisfaction of having born and bred a family, I've not experienced the conscious deprivation of motherhood. Like many others, I would have had to learn how to be a mother and I think I would have had to have the right man at my side to do so. But at night in my dreams, I am an instinctive earth mother. I can be counted on. I give life strongly and tenderly.

My recurrent baby dreams have become far less frequent since Taller San Jose came into being. So was Taller San Jose the baby that was waiting to be born within me? Were the recurrent dreams an insistent reminder that I had love and life to give that I had not yet delivered? I am much more of a mother now than I have ever been—to my young staff and to the young men and women who now inhabit my daily life.

Mothering well is a gift, I think. I try not to make judgments about the mothering skills of the young women who come through our doors—not even in my head, but I can't help but notice how a baby is touched and cuddled and talked to. I see when a baby is handled like a sack of potatoes, set aside like an inanimate object, or when a five-year-old is left in the dust without a hand to cling to. I notice how young women talk about their children and pull out their pictures and how others don't mention them at all.

When I am talking with a young mother and she never mentions her child, I get the feeling that the baby is like a parcel that she has left at home—that she will pick up when she returns. And so in conversation, I bring the baby into the present moment and place the child between us.

"How's your baby?" I ask in an interested, casual manner.

"Oh, fine," she'll say. No big deal.

You've got to feel loved to pass it on, I think. I've got to love this person in front of me right now whether she's a great mother or not.

Some young women have babies too soon in life—pregnant at thirteen, a mom at fourteen. They come back to school at eighteen or nineteen with a four- or five-year-old child in tow and maybe a baby or two more to care for. They've been mothering for years now and they're tired; at times they want to forget their role and responsibilities and step into the life of a school girl again—carefree, without ties and burdens. Sometimes when they give birth in their early teens, their own mothers rear the children and they watch from the sidelines, helpers but without full responsibility.

"Do you have children?" I'll say.

"Oh yes, I have two—well, really three, but the oldest one, he's with my mother, sometimes I forget that he's mine." Her mother, the one who cleans buildings at night and cares for her grandchild during the day, I doubt that she forgets. And does the child know who he belongs to? When he turns eleven or twelve and the gang offers an elusive sense of family and the certainty of belonging to someone or something—I wonder who he'll turn to then?

There is only one time that I longed to be a mother and it was because of the grace and the love that I witnessed between a mother and her daughter at the Oakland airport. It was because I was traveling alone that I had the opportunity to gawk about me and study the other passengers and to note the relationships between and among them. A mother and her teenage daughter drew most of my attention. It was late August, and the girl was leaving for her first semester in college. The mother and daughter alternated between checking airline tickets, papers, and forms and throwing quick tender looks at each other. Just before the mother's fond gaze would threaten to arouse tears in the daughter, the girl would break eye contact and fiddle with her purse or her ticket. When the rows were called for boarding, I stood behind the two of them in line. I felt strangely invested in their relationship. A minute before their final parting, the mother grabbed her daughter squarely by the shoulders, fixed her eyes on her child, and spoke to her directly in a calm, firm voice.

"You are my most precious child," she said. "You are ready for this new adventure. And I will always be here for you. I want you to remember that there is nothing—*nothing* that you can ever do that will separate you from my love. Do you understand that?"

They embraced each other in tears and I, too, began to cry. I would have liked to have been that kind of mother. The young people that I work with need that kind of love.

During the day, I try to love each person in front of me and I consciously ask for the grace to share in the all-embracing love of God. And then by night, when judgment is no longer an issue, I rescue forgotten babies in my sleep.

CHAPTER THIRTEEN

*Holding my tears…it didn't make me stronger. It made me
cautious to the emotions that I face everyday of my life.*
                                                    —Juan Carrasco

Five years after Taller San Jose opened, I took off for the
abbey. Although our program was fruitful and growing, something was amiss within me. I'd begun to forget appointments and
to let deadlines slide. Worse, I'd forgotten to notice whether or
not the sun had risen or set. Everyday I was becoming more tired,
less imaginative. I craved minutes, hours, and days to myself. I
was soul-weary and I had begun to be filled with self-doubt. I
didn't know if I had the ability to provide leadership to the rap-
idly growing Taller San Jose. The issues that the young people
faced were complex and culturally bound and the magnitude of
their problems sometimes overwhelmed me.

The constant pressure of raising funds to support the program was wearing me down. I suspected that I had begun to feel
a bit like the young people I was trying to help—frequently worried about money. I fretted about cash flow problems before I
went to sleep and I thought about them again when I awakened.
I feared that I wouldn't be able to support what I had so boldly
begun.

People will laugh at me, I thought—at my naiveté, the fact
that I had built a house on sand and had no way to support it. *But
it was only my pride that would suffer, I consoled myself. We've been
able to help a lot of kids and keep a number of them from returning to
jail; isn't that enough?* Still, day after day there was an endless
stream of young people coming through the door and I didn't
have the heart to turn them away.

I asked God for faith and trust—the kind that Mother Teresa had often talked about with humble clarity. My faith and trust were not as strong as hers, so I asked God for a concrete sign, some certainty that Taller San Jose was going to survive without my constant pedaling. I felt an urgent need to take some time off, not to vacation, but to grow quiet and to rest my soul. I wanted to take stock of all that had happened since I had moved to Santa Ana, to make certain that I wasn't losing myself in frenetic activity. I wasn't a social worker, after all. I was first and foremost a Catholic nun. I longed to spend some time alone in a holy place, but I wanted to be certain that if I was to take some time off, that I wasn't going to leave the organization in jeopardy.

One bright day in June 2000, I opened the morning mail to learn that the California Endowment had awarded Taller San Jose a grant of $600,000. I was ecstatic. I knew that our work would continue.

A few weeks later I was sitting on a mountaintop with the Trappistine nuns in Sonoita, Arizona. When I made the turn from the highway onto the winding dirt road leading to their abbey, I experienced excitement and fear. Excitement, because I believed that I was in for an adventure; scared, because I never knew what message God had in mind for me when I chose to empty the clutter of my soul and to sit quite still and listen.

The little abbey, dwarfed by ranges of high purple mountains, huddled under the ever-changing skies of southwestern Arizona. My small room was soothing and clean. I was seeking solitude and there was plenty of it to be found. There was no television. Neither were there newspapers. I had no access to the Internet and my transistor radio would only pick up stations from Mexico. I had brought a cell phone with me for emergencies but it didn't have the power to transmit across the 9,000 foot peaks of the Santa Rita Mountains. The phone in the abbey had been knocked out by an electrical storm several weeks before. Solitude cloaked the mountaintop and encircled me in its embrace.

The Trappistine nuns went quietly about their work each day—gathering at appointed times to celebrate the liturgy or to pray the psalms. I was free to join them whenever I wanted. The quiet rhythm of their days gave structure to my own. During my first two weeks there, I slept a great deal. I had a deep thirst in my soul. Like someone who had crossed the desert without water, I drank deeply of spiritual books and solitude and liturgy and prayer. I hesitated to call my time away a spiritual retreat. I associated regularity and frequent prayer with a time of retreat. I didn't want the pressure and expectation of performing set spiritual practices or of praying on schedule. I just wanted to be in a holy place and among people who were praying. Looking back, I can see that I was a spiritual invalid in a recovery home. I needed to lean on others for my support.

One morning when I was out walking at some distance from the abbey, I watched a large black crow take flight from out of the grey stillness. I could hear the swish of his wings for a very long time. As he circled and gained speed, he kept a bead on the ground, looking for some tasty desert morsel to devour. Every few seconds he let out a loud caw and then from nowhere a soul mate joined him. They danced together in the sky as they ascended higher and higher and then they disappeared into the heavens.

Just as I lost sight of the birds, a rifle sounded from a distant canyon and the deafening noise set the monastery dogs to barking. Suddenly I was in Santa Ana again where the gunshots broke the peace each night and where the neighborhood dogs bayed until one or another signaled that it was safe to stop.

At night, in the solitude of my room, the young people from Santa Ana came to visit me in my dreams. Sergio, the first to appear, sputtered and stammered his troubles to me in both English and Spanish. The next night Marie fell into my arms and wept, confiding to me that she was pregnant with her fourth child, a child that she and her young husband could ill afford. One night it was Miguel who awakened me with worry, sharing the troublesome news that he was living in the back of a truck and paying a householder to use the bathroom—except that now he had no more money. And finally, Enríque walked into my dreams. Enríque, whose father had killed his mother and then turned the gun on himself, had been left an orphan—with his brother, both of them in detention facilities when they learned of their parents' deaths. Now he, the older brother, was scratching to make a living for the two of them and to rent a cheap room that would become the family home. The sad dreams, worrisome images merged with reality, left me feeling helpless and strangely shaken.

How had these young people slipped into the backpack of my unconscious? I hadn't known that they'd smuggled themselves in among my simple belongings. I hadn't asked for the dreams, but they revealed to me how much I take in from each student, how their stories affect me and how I carry them in my heart even when I'm far away.

The life of the Trappistines was attractive to me. I envied the prescribed pace of their days, the predictability of it all. I had entered the convent, after all, to seek God and from time to time over the years I wondered if I'd lost my way along the path. The concerns that filled my days at Taller San Jose often turned into preoccupations and worries. Although I was convinced that I was doing the Lord's work, I longed to do it with love, grace, humility, peace, and joy. Oftentimes I was far off the mark.

When I joined the Trappistines for prayers, I imagined myself living as they did—a calmer, more regulated life. I could grow used to the schedule, I thought, and the quiet. But at the end of Vespers each day, when they prayed for the world, for family and friends, for the hurting and the poor, it was my joy to silently mouth the names of the young people that I carried in my heart. I knew then that I wanted to know the names of those for whom I prayed. I wanted to see their faces before me. Much as I admired the Trappistines, I didn't belong on this hill. God had asked me to walk another path.

"God is not exclusive," a wise monk once said. "He is all-inclusive. God can be found within and in the quiet of the cell. But he cannot *not* be found in others and in all and still be found within and in the quiet of the cell. We cannot be selective as to where we are going to find God. God is where He is."

While God had been with me on the mountain top, even more so I knew that God had been with me at Taller San Jose and that's where I needed to return, where I could put faces and names on those for whom I prayed.

Just after I returned from Arizona, I met Mario Pineda and I added his name to my prayer list. I can't remember exactly what Mario's goals were when he first found his way to Taller San Jose. He didn't achieve any of them while he was with us. I think he was stoned most of the time, but he denied it when I asked him. Mario was nineteen when I first met him and kind of a lost soul, even among his peers. He wanted some place to belong and so he hung out with us. He wasn't obnoxious; he didn't have an attitude, but he looked meaner than sin and his mouth turned downward in a permanent scowl. We were doing a lot of building renovation when Mario came on board and he got right in and worked alongside us—provided we were generous with the pizza and donuts.

Whoever first designed the Taller San Jose building in the 1920s had an eye for beautiful woodwork. Over the years the once elegant crown molding, window sashes, and detailing had been buried under multiple layers of thick enamel paint. The top-coat was a nondescript beige. I wanted to restore the natural wood beneath it and so I put the guys to work with paint stripper and small wire brushes. It was tedious work, especially around the ox-eye window with its delicate wood-framed design. The intricate window could only be reached from a tall ladder. Mario was my window man.

Mario had one prevailing belief—that the care and grooming of his hair was key to his advancement in life—to success, money, girls, and employment. He monkeyed with his hair constantly. He could tell me the exact setting for the buzz jobs he required—the sides, the top, the back. It all looked shaved to me. He experimented with color and settled on an orangey bronze. It wasn't a color that God intended for hair, but Mario liked it. Every week there would be a new twist, though he had hardly any hair to work with at all.

One day, Mario was more jittery than usual and toward the end of the day he confided to me that there was a warrant out for his arrest and that he was to turn himself in by 4:00 p. m. That meant the Santa Ana jail—about four blocks down the street. Mario hadn't been in jail before and I could see that he was scared. He looked a lot tougher than he was. He hadn't committed any violent crimes; his offenses were related to traffic violations. He'd been driving without a license and been cited several times. If he didn't turn himself in, they were going to come after him. Mario paced up and down in front of our building for about two hours in the late afternoon. He just couldn't make himself do it. He couldn't make himself do much of anything. I think it was the pot that took away his *ganas*. It smothered his fears, suppressed his dreams, and robbed him of the will to act in his own regard.

After that, I didn't see Mario for months. He just disappeared.

❦

There are some plants in the Sonoran desert that disappear when times are tough. In extreme drought, when rain has been scarce for years, these rugged shrubs cling to life by going underground, surviving in seed form and in darkness until it's safe to come out again. They sustain themselves for years this way, breaking ground only when they sense that the outer world holds no threat for them. An innate wisdom governs their strategy. These hardy plants are not the kind that one is tempted to pick or to paint. Actually, they're scrappy, raspy weeds. Their glory and their strength is in their tough roots.

I think that young people like Mario must share something in common with these rough, desert plants. They grow up in families and in neighborhoods that are tough on survival. These young people seek nurturance wherever and whenever they can find it—an ounce of support can be as scarce as a drop of water on the hot desert floor. Sometimes they make poor choices. Then they hide out for long periods of time in darkness, in underworlds where drugs and crime are rampant. Not everyone makes it to adulthood in this setting and even those that do don't always get to participate fully in the good life or the American dream.

✦✦✦

The next time I saw Mario, I barely recognized him. He had grown a mustache, a goatee, and arched his eyebrows. He was still obsessed with the power of hair. He'd also added a couple of piercings to his ears and nose. He looked like the devil himself and I told him so.

"*¡A mi, te pareces como un diablo!*"

But he liked the look. He thought it gave him character. He was working now and had a girlfriend. He just wanted to let me know how he was doing.

"Great, Mario, I'm glad to hear the goods news." I hardly knew what more to say. He didn't look like any son I'd be proud to claim, but at least he was reporting in and I was grateful for that.

I've learned over time that a number of kids use Taller San Jose as their touchstone for growth, their symbol of hope, even if they don't achieve the goals that I would like for them and on my schedule. Like Mario, they come back to report success. Often they come back when they've hit the bottom and are scared. I've learned not to measure progress in a straight line. I want them to come back anytime, whatever the story.

Months later, Mario appeared again just as I returned from a meeting at St. Joseph Hospital. I was eager to get back to work and to the tasks that had backed up on my desk throughout the morning. When I got out of my van, I knew that my agenda had already changed. A skinny kid was pacing back and forth in front of the building. I didn't recognize him at first. It was Mario. He'd lost about thirty pounds since I'd seen him last—that's a lot on a small frame. He looked emaciated and very distressed.

"Do you have a minute?" he asked. I knew that it would take an hour.

"For you, always, *Precioso*," I answered, rearranging my afternoon agenda. I made no comment about his shriveled state.

When we sat down in my office he started to cry, to sob. His girlfriend had left him. He was distraught beyond measure. He would do anything to get her back. He'd treated her so well. She'd found a new guy. The new guy didn't know how to treat her, how to take care of her. Mario couldn't eat, couldn't sleep. He was stalking her. Obsessed. He thought he might kill himself.

Mario was worried about himself. I was worried about Mario.

I've learned that there is no sense trying to refer a young person for further counseling or any other intervention unless the situation is life-threatening in the extreme and then it's a matter for the police. Mario had mustered all his courage to talk to me. He wasn't going to talk to anybody else right now. He was placing his life in my hands.

My training in counseling had taught me how to assess for potential suicide—or homicide, for that matter. Mario was clearly distressed, outrageously so—despondent enough to take his own life. I wondered if he felt the same about the life of his girlfriend or her new man.

Did he have the means to harm himself or another? I needed to know this.

Negative.

Did he have a plan to do so?

He hadn't thought about that.

Had he ever acted in violence before—toward himself, another?

I asked my questions in a soft conversational mode, but I needed the answers.

Mario was indeed profoundly depressed. Through our conversation, I learned that his deep despair was turned inward. He was more likely to harm himself than another.

Mario then confided to me that he still had some penalty related to his outstanding warrants from the past. He could either pay the fines, which were substantial, and for which he now had the money or he could spend a week in jail and save his money.

"If I'm in jail, I'll feel safer," he admitted. "I won't hurt myself in jail. I'll be around other people."

I was shocked. It seemed a radical solution but one which he had puzzled out himself. It made sense to him. He made a firm decision to turn himself in.

"Do you want to pray?" I asked, before he left. He nodded yes. I blessed him on the forehead with holy water. I told him that the water was to remind him of his baptism, when God chose him as his special son forever. I asked God's protection upon him. Tears rolled down his cheeks—and mine, too.

⚹

Several months later Mario wandered in to my office looking better than I'd seen him in a long time.

"I got my driver's license back," he boasted, "and I opened a bank account."

I wonder if he knew how happy he made me. We have seven important objectives at Taller San Jose and we emphasize them at every turn. Having a driver's license and using a bank account are important ones. Finishing high school, staying out of jail, learning how to use a computer, and getting a job are equally important. Registering to vote, if you can, finishes off the list and makes you a card-carrying American citizen.

While I thought Mario had accomplished nothing at Taller San Jose, he actually had heard the "steps to success" and committed them to memory. He was proud of his accomplishments. In addition, he had a job—and one that he liked. He had earned his certificate as a nursing assistant and he was working in a convalescent hospital. He liked helping people. He felt needed. He was making good money—$9.00 an hour.

He confided to me that day that his mother looked down on his work and called him an "ass washer." He wanted to know what I thought.

"We need more ass washers, *Precioso*," I answered. "Most of us will reach a time in our lives when we need someone to help us. We'll all need our asses washed at some point. It's tough to be feeble or sick and not to be able to take care of yourself. Your work has a lot of dignity. I'm proud of you."

I was very proud of Mario and humbled to be a small part of his life.

❧❀❧

A year passed before I talked with Mario again. This time it was a phone call.

"Sister Eileen," he announced as if we had just talked yesterday. "It's Mario."

"What's going on?" I asked, cautiously. I wondered if he was in trouble again, depressed, or needed help.

"I just called to tell you that I have a baby—a girl—and I'm married. I'm doing okay. I'm really happy. Can I bring my baby by to show you?"

"Anytime, *Precioso*." I hung up, content to start the day. I wondered if Mario knew how much he filled me with hope, what a privilege it had been for me to stand in the wings and watch him grow. And now he was bringing his firstborn for a visit.

Does that make me a grandmother? I wondered. *Surely I'm old enough.*

⛧

I work with young people who carry insufferable burdens of brokenness and pain. But it's not as if they are the wounded ones and I am the healer. I am broken too. I humbly ask God to make me aware of my weak points, my blind spots, the hidden traps that feed my need for vanity and power. I ask for the grace to see those flaws in me that all my friends (and coworkers!) know so well and that I alone seem to be unaware of. I ask for the grace to change my stubborn, opinionated self even at this late stage in my life.

Do I want to be zapped by grace in such a way that I will be a completely different person? Sometimes, in a crazy unrealistic way, I want that to happen. It seems easier than the slow growth path toward humility and self-knowledge. I'd like God to replace all the broken parts within me with healthier ways of being, thinking, acting, and loving. But over the years, I have learned that God does not work with me in that way. He teaches me from my experience, and that is always distressingly grounded and painstakingly incremental. The same is true of kids like Mario. They're blessed if they can learn from their experience.

⛧

When I first meet these young people, they are soul-weary from life's adversities and burdened by worries and troubles long before they have the strength to carry them. The carefree innocence of their youth is long gone and *joie de vivre* if they ever had it, is all but extinguished within them. They don't giggle and laugh as young people are meant to do. Instead, they trudge forward weighed down by imaginary backpacks filled with stones. Middle-aged worries already draw their dark eyes downward. These young people, skipping through childhood too quickly, have often dug deep pits of trouble for themselves or else raw poverty has pushed them facedown into its fateful mire. Broken in spirit, they are often stuck so far down in hopelessness and woe that it is impossible for them to climb out and upward on their own. They're not even sure if life is worth the struggle.

There is an old coral tree on the grounds in a nearby park and when I pass the tree, it speaks to me of primal struggle. Early in its growth cycle, the old tree's two central branches separated from the trunk—perhaps when the tree was still a seedling. The arms of the great tree parted just inches from the ground and instead of heading skyward as branches are meant to do, the heavy boughs leaned down upon the ground, surrendering themselves to the forces of gravity.

"We just can't," the branches must have sighed one night when no one in particular was listening. "It's tough being a tree and no one is showing us how to grow up. We yield to the power of least resistance."

And so at some point in its tender youth, the tree just sat down upon itself and gave up. Now its twisted appendages rest upon the earth and the leaves of the tree shoot upward from their curious, humbled state. It is a beautiful tree in an odd sort of way—but thwarted. When I walk past the old tree, I ask it what happened in its formative years that it relinquished its power and dreams so quickly.

In spite of all that I have come to understand about the barrio and the young people who grow up in poverty, I ask this same question of them. "Why do you give up your power and your dreams so quickly?"

Every year we go around the neighborhoods to find the city's youth—the ones who have given up on life too soon. We always visit the churches—not because the young are there but because many of their mothers and grandmothers are faithful church-goers.

"Is there any young person in your household that you're

worried about?" we ask in Spanish, borrowing a minute of pulpit time. "Anyone who hasn't finished school, who doesn't have a job, or who is in trouble?"

And then there is a stirring in the forest of worshippers. Heads bob up and down like a multitude of tree boughs caught one after the other by the same sudden gush of hope.

"Help us," their eyes, like dark sad knotholes plead. "Our children are dying."

"For there is hope for a tree," says Job. *"[I]f it is cut down, that it will sprout again, and that its shoots will not cease. Though its root grows old in the earth, and its stump dies in the ground, yet at the scent of water it will bud and put forth branches like a young plant"* (Job 14:7–9). That's what I believe. I believe in watering damaged, young trees. When tended with love, they can start their lives anew.

CHAPTER FOURTEEN

I know that I prematurely made a lot of decisions that will affect my destiny.

—Juan Carrasco

I met Mona Gomez when she was five months pregnant and very edgy. She had just turned eighteen and her boyfriend Ivan, the father of her child, was in jail. Ivan had beaten Mona so badly that she landed in the hospital. The first time that he wreaked his rage upon her, she lost the baby that she was carrying.

Sometimes people think that it's only the guys who are gang members, only the guys who get in trouble and land in jail, but that's not true. Mona Gomez was in deep trouble by the time she was fifteen. Mona was an independent and headstrong young woman. She railed against her parents' every rule. A textbook on delinquency would label her "oppositional."

When Mona decided to attach herself to Ivan, no intervention of her parents or the school truant officer could keep her from him. Ivan had led Mona down a sordid path. He involved her in his gang activities and shared his drug life with her—pot, cocaine, and heroin. She left high school shortly after she met him and she began to follow his destructive path. When he had dragged her down far enough, he called her a *puta*—a degrading term in Spanish and a word that doesn't sound too good in English either.

"How did you find your way to Taller San Jose?" I asked her one day.

"My father read about it in the newspaper," she answered. "He thought I might be interested in the nurse's aide class here and so he drove me over and signed me up."

Mona was tense, guarded, jumpy. She was back living with her family but she wasn't sure who she was or to whom she belonged. Deep down, she was still Ivan's girl.

In spite of the massive abuse that she had suffered, Mona had a fierce loyalty to Ivan. He was, after all, she said "the father of my child."

Away from Ivan's daily presence, his putdowns and abuse, color slowly crept back into Mona's cheeks and light began to shine in her eyes. She did well in class and when it was time for supervised clinical experience caring for real patients in the convalescent hospital, Mona instinctively knew what to do. She wasn't put off by frailty, senility, or the humble but necessary tasks involved in bathing and attending to the hygienic needs of those who are helpless. Mona found dignity in the work and she began to hold her head higher.

At the June graduation, Mona was nine months pregnant. It hadn't been an easy time; her emotions had been erratic. The baby was born small and frail. I visited Mona when the baby came home from the hospital and that was the day that I met the family dog, Toro.

Toro was not actually a pet; he was a fierce sentinel—poised to protect Mona when she didn't have the sense to protect herself. Toro was an Akita, tall and muscular, with a large well-shaped head and piercing blue eyes. His deep growl started far back in his throat, rumbled through the neighborhood with the fury of a volcano and then burst forth in a menacing roar. The Akita is a natural guard dog. With this breed, protecting master and turf are instinctual. I've always been a great lover of dogs, but Toro struck a chord of fear within me that day. I knew that he was there to protect Mona from Ivan, but I was afraid of him too.

❧

At the end of the summer, I asked Mona if she would speak about her life and experience at Taller San Jose's annual fundraising gala. In spite of having been beaten down and trampled upon, Mona was vibrant, articulate, and expressive. She had the ability to communicate with a large crowd—a challenging task at best. Mona eagerly accepted the opportunity and we spent some time together planning what she might say. I told her that the night before the event, I wanted to go over her speech with her, giving her some practice and coaching her on how to throw her voice to reach the farthest recesses of the crowd.

I agreed to pick up Mona at 6:00 p.m. on Friday evening before the Saturday event and drive her to the Motherhouse in Orange for the final practice. I called her just before I left my house to let her know that I would be at her door within five minutes.

The family dog, Toro, was waiting for me when I arrived. He stood in front of the door—silent, strong, steady, alert, wide-eyed. His collar was fixed to a long chain. The doorbell was to the right behind him. There was no sign of Mona.

There was no way I was going to get around Toro to Mona's front door without divine intervention—that, mixed with a degree of caution. If I thought about the situation too long, I knew that Toro would smell the fear that was already leaking from my pores. I followed advice that I had read regarding encounters with fierce dogs. *Don't look them in the eye*, it said. *They'll think you are challenging them.* I glanced quickly away.

In a flash, I was on the ground, a hot searing pain shooting through my side. The giant dog was all over me. I screamed a scream that I had been storing for decades—rallying the living and dead to my aid.

The Gomez family were the first to arrive. They pulled Toro off and hurried me inside. I put on my strong act. Cool.

"Sorry to have scared you," I apologized.

Ivan sat in the middle of the room, shirtless. His body was well muscled from his prison workouts. Elaborate tattoos covered his chest and arms. He had Toro's teeth. Baby Vanessa sat on her father's lap.

Dang, I thought sadly. *She's got Ivan's face.*

I negated all offers of assistance.

"Just a scratch," I said.

Meanwhile, my insides were quivering. I was shaky all over and the pain was intense. I asked for a couple of Tylenol. I used the family bathroom and pulled up my blouse to survey the damage. Blood oozed in several places from where Toro's magnificent teeth had punctured my flesh. I felt nauseous and weak. I leaned over the sink and slowly took in deep draughts of air to calm myself.

In shock, I focused on the task at hand—Mona's practice session in Orange. Mona had not yet finished nursing her eight-week-old baby. I would wait.

"Take all the time you need." I sipped a glass of water and feigned a patience I did not feel.

I sat on the couch and stared at Ivan. I wanted to get Mona away from Ivan, now, permanently.

When Mona and I arrived at the Motherhouse, my common sense advisors hurried me to St. Joseph's Hospital emergency room. I had lost my glasses in the scuffle. At the triage station, I squinted at the line marked *reason for visit* and penciled in the words "dog bite." If I had had presence of mind and the ability to see clearly, I would have written, "severe mauling by massive dog." Toro hadn't just taken a bite out of my side but also my pride. I later learned that he had nibbled his way down my body and ended his tirade by shredding the legs of my denim pants.

I took my turn amidst a long line of patients waiting for treatment on that busy Friday night. While I waited, I invented headlines to announce my demise—*Santa Ana nun mauled by vicious dog...Well-meaning nun felled by massive canine.*

The Taller San Jose fundraising event was a raving success. In a daze, I greeted the nearly five hundred guests. I was careful to greet all the guests at arm's distance; I couldn't bear for anyone to touch me.

Poised, Mona spoke earnestly and confidently that night about the opportunity that she had had to graduate with her nurse aide certification. Her next step was to get a job, she proclaimed and that's exactly what she did.

The guard dog, Toro, is still at his post.

CHAPTER FIFTEEN

I don't see freedom. I still see chains tied to my hands. As I try to break them, they get tighter on me.

—Juan Carrasco

When Ricardo and Ruben, two of our wood workers, tested dirty for drugs, I was profoundly disappointed. I guess I thought they had been doing just fine. I don't like to think of myself as naïve, but I don't want to be suspicious all the time either. So if our young men showed up on time everyday and were good workers I presumed they were doing okay. It wasn't always so. It was their probation officer who informed me of the dirty drug test. And so I had to let them go—at least for the moment. It was our policy. If they were willing to meet with a drug counselor and actively work on drug free behavior they could come back. Otherwise, they couldn't work for us—it was a safety issue, a matter of integrity. All the guys knew who was using and when. I was the one who was sometimes in the dark.

Ruben couldn't remember a life without drugs. His father died of a heroin overdose when he was four years old and his mother has been in and out of jail for drug sales. His older brothers introduced him to pot before he was ten years old. From that point on, he was involved in the dirty, family business. He doesn't remember that it was ever a choice. It was how the family lived and they taught him everything they knew.

He didn't like selling drugs so it was his role to steal. He got good at it but in his heart he knew it was wrong. "I got used to it," he said, "and after a while it was easy, but I always wanted out. I just couldn't find the way."

It was his probation officer who suggested that he try out Taller San Jose, finish his education there, and learn some skills.

I knew that both Ruben and Ricardo would be reluctant to meet with the drug counselor. It just wasn't in their culture to do so. They didn't readily own up to their sins or admit vulnerability. Besides, she was a woman. They were macho kind of guys and talking about real feelings with a woman would be a first-class emotional stretch.

We were to be involved in a garden show at Mission San Juan Capistrano that weekend—a booth to show our benches and hopefully sell a few. In spite of the fact that I'd dismissed Ricardo and Ruben as workers, I had chosen them for my helpers on Saturday. I figured that if I had them with me all day, I might be able to persuade them to get some help for themselves and get back on track.

They agreed to accompany me and I arranged to pick them up at Ricardo's house. Ruben would never let me pick him up at his apartment.

"I don't want you to see where I live," he'd say. "It's really bad."

I knew the street. It was ugly. Some of our other students lived there too, but I honored his wishes. I didn't push it. He said he'd meet me at Ricardo's.

I pulled into Ricardo's driveway at 9:00 a.m. and rang the doorbell. No answer. I knocked. When there was no response, I walked to the back of the house to see if anyone was around. I didn't see a sign of life and I was growing impatient, already fussed with the guys for their drug use. Just as I was about to give up on both of them, Ruben arrived in his pale blue '72 Chevy— the longest car in the city of Santa Ana. Ruben was eager and ready to go. He led me around to the back of the house and he knocked on Ricardo's bedroom window. Then he pulled off the screen. We both stuck our heads inside. Ricardo was groggy from sleep and not at all interested in getting up.

Probably using again last night, I thought. *He's strung out, hung over.*

I mustered my strongest tone of voice though I probably sounded like weak pudding, "Ricardo, you have five minutes to get up and get dressed."

He took twenty. We headed off to the mission forty-five minutes late, but I was glad to have them both in tow. A crew from Taller San Jose had arrived before us and the benches and chairs were displayed under the spread of an elm tree. The boys and I sat in the shade of the tree and I attempted to pump Ricardo and Ruben full of wisdom, hope, and *my* motivation. I explained the employee assistance program to them again and what it meant—drug testing for cause, meeting with a trained addiction counselor, participation in a twelve-step program. If they wanted to keep their jobs, there was one option: either participate in the program or we would be forced to cut them loose from employment. They had twenty-four hours to think about it.

In the end, Ruben agreed to my terms and to participate in the drug-counseling program.

Ricardo cut his ties at the workplace; I didn't see him for a long while. I was sad to see him leave. There was something innately good about him and even at eighteen, he was a charmer. I tried to imagine him ten years later as a husband and father. I hoped that he wouldn't waste the decade away on drugs. I invited him to keep in touch.

In the first years at Taller San Jose, I could sometimes act as a codependent mother hen. I didn't want to lose any of the young people who came to us. I was tolerant of behavior that I should have challenged. I've since learned to hold them to a higher standard and asked the staff to do the same. If we don't, who will?

Ruben did participate in the drug program and he began to attend twelve-step meetings, but it was hard. He lived with his family in a crowded one bedroom apartment. Everyone in the apartment used heroin and everyday he was surrounded by drugs.

When I saw him slowing down, sleeping on the job, I excused him at first. I was tired; maybe he was tired. But forty years separated us in age. I understood my fatigue, but a twenty-year-old kid should rightfully be filled with energy. Over time Ruben began to drift back into drugs and we had to dismiss him from the workforce.

I wrote to him on his last day at work.

> *You know, Ruben, that my worry about you is your on-going use of drugs and alcohol and what that does to mess you up. Why I worry, is that I've seen guys really mess themselves up around here and end up back in jail when they never thought it would happen to them. Drugs and alcohol change how you see the world and the decisions that you make and how you treat people. I'm not saying that no one should ever drink, but you have to look at what kind of trouble you get into when you're drinking and using. Even if you don't think that AA and NA work for you now, remember that those programs are always there to offer you support. Don't ever be afraid to come by and say "hi" to folks here. Nobody's mad at you. I care about you very much. Until I see you again, Ruben, please remember that I keep you in my prayers each day. I will ask God to help you find the right job and help you stay clean and safe and strong inside. God made you and He cares about you very much—don't ever forget that.*

Three weeks later Ruben was back in jail. He'd been arrested for driving without a license and for drug possession and he was court-ordered to attend a drug program for ninety days— it was a chance for recovery. He did well in the program. It was thirty miles from his home and no one in his family visited him. He obeyed all the rules and regulations of the recovery program, attending twelve-step meetings every day. After a month, when he was allowed some discretionary time, he drove back up to Taller San Jose to report in and to tell us how well he was doing. He looked good; he had put on some weight and he wore a broad smile. He was filled with images and stories about the other men in the program—the older, wasted ones who had spent years in jail, on the streets, and intermittently in drug recovery programs. He didn't want that kind of life, he proclaimed. He was learning to stay clean and he was proud of his progress.

I know that a lot of our students have a history of drug use. Just studying the pattern of their high school years tells me that. They enroll in the local high school in their freshman year and somewhere along the line they drift to the continuation school. In neither school setting do they earn enough credits to graduate. They develop a pattern of enrolling and not finishing what they start. They are known as "double dropouts." Either they are kicked out of school for behavioral problems or they attend less and less frequently so that at some point the school system has to caution them that they will not earn a diploma. The school system is legally responsible for them until they are eighteen, and so they drift from one dropout program to another and finally out onto the streets. Although not all of the students who follow this pattern are drug users, many are. When you're using drugs, even intermittently, the motivation to achieve and to accomplish diminishes. There is a restlessness about life, an inability to sit still and concentrate. It isn't hard to spot this pattern among students who enroll at Taller San Jose.

We confront and challenge what we view as drug-related behaviors—frequent absence and tardiness, sleeping in class, erratic mood swings, and the inability to follow through on commitments. We can't refer those we suspect to be chronic drug users for jobs; we'd have hell to pay with employers. Drugs—our dirty national problem is a chronic affliction among out-of-school Hispanic youth. It is their undoing; it robs them of their *ganas*—that peculiar Mexican grace that fuels the soul.

❦

Sometimes, in the morning, when I am making my way from my bedroom to our kitchen for my first cup of coffee, I pass our quiet, empty living room. I fantasize filling it with young people like Ruben for the night. I think that if I could just bring some of them back to the convent at night that I could keep them safe.

You'll have to come home with me, I practice telling them in a firm, motherly tone. *I want you to live with me until you're grown up and stronger. The world out there isn't good for you. It's filled with dangerous traps. I'll keep you safe here in the convent for a while.*

And then on my way back to my bedroom, coffee in hand, I am jolted back to reality. *This is crazy-nun talk,* I think, *I'm not their keeper.* I can't do it all and even if I could protect these young people in the quiet safety of the convent overnight, there's not room for everyone. And in time they would view me as their jailer, grow to resent my rules, my structure, and my smothering, mothering care. It would be as if they were imprisoned by a kindly but suffocating grandmother, taught to appreciate soft music and made to watch her favorite TV shows and forced to learn how to crochet and to do watercolors and to pray.

CHAPTER SIXTEEN

I thank God for still having me alive, because if it wasn't for him I would be dead. After eight years of gang life, drugs and alcohol, I'm still alive. People said I wouldn't make it. People said I would die.

—David Flores

I carry a picture of my Irish grandfather, Joseph Casey, in my wallet. He was dead when I was born. I only know him through my mother, his daughter, and she didn't have a high opinion of him. I know that he drank to excess and that he abused my grandmother. I know that when family emergencies arose—like the frequent illnesses of his small son, he could not handle the pain and wandered away. Joseph Casey died when he was forty-one—alone in a motel room. His heart stopped. His son had died the year before; my mother, his only daughter, had left for nursing school the previous weekend and he had just left his wife—again—with seventeen cents to her name.

In the photo that was passed on to me, my grandfather is pictured as a young, shabbily dressed railroad man—an unskilled laborer. The men who surround him in the photo share a common demeanor—a harsh and hungry look. They are young men burdened by cares too early in life. Joseph Casey was the oldest son of immigrant parents. My great-grandparents had come from Ireland in the latter part of the nineteenth century because there was no way for them to survive on that cold, rocky island. My grandfather was an undereducated young man trying to make his way between the world of his parents and their new-found land. Although Joseph Casey was born in America, he never found his footing here. There were Americans who had come before him who didn't care much for his type. The "New World" didn't always welcome the Irish, labeling them both dirty and feisty. It was a world in which the sign "No Irish Need Apply" was commonly posted by employers. In this harsh environment, Joseph Casey was not blessed with strong coping skills. Among second-generation immigrants, I doubt that he was alone in his weakness. When life is tough a number of people fall to the bottom of the heap, scarcely noticed and sometimes trampled upon as the tide of life inexorably marches on.

I wish that my grandfather had led a stronger and happier life—that he had survived long enough for me to have known him. His dysfunction and sadness visited itself upon both my grandmother and my mother. I want the young people that I am working with today, the children of the immigrant poor, to do better than my grandfather did; I want them to do more than merely survive. Many of them are already parents and the quality of their lives will profoundly affect their children and perhaps the next generation as well.

I don't know what lies ahead for the young people who have shared their stories with me, but I am privileged to know them and like the best of parents, I want to give them both roots and wings.

I often think about the most troubled young people that I meet as the lost sheep, the ones that Jesus talked about in the scriptures. These are the sheep that stray from the flock as it moves ahead, the ones that get caught in the brambles and thorns and then become easy prey for the ever-present wolves.

When I picture Jesus, the Good Shepherd, I imagine him walking calmly amidst the bramble bushes, staff in hand, freeing the lambs from their entrapment and carrying them back to the flock, one at a time, across his broad capable shoulders. I don't know how far he had to walk to rescue his errant lambs or what the rest of the flock was doing in his absence. Maybe the Good Shepherd was frantic at times, worried about both the wayward lambs and the safety of the larger flock left under the protection of the sheep dogs.

I myself am more of a sheep dog than a shepherd. I've only seen these energetic border collies in the movies. I remember them leaping about, running ahead, circling the flock, and holding off potential strays with their intense gaze. Surely these worker-dogs are exhausted by nightfall. They lie at the feet of their master, every fiber of their being spent in his service, yet ready to leap into action again at his ready signal.

That's me, the sheep dog. It is my way of guarding the flock. I involve myself in endless frantic activities to keep the lambs safe and growing. I attend meetings. I beg for money. I explore potential opportunities. I'm in and out of the classrooms, up and down the hallways, noting who is present and if they're happy, engaged, focused. I'm all over town doing my job. Like the border collie, I do it by instinct but I'm not always certain that I choose the right activities or that my efforts are fruitful. I know that I am very tired at night—soul-tired. It's my soul that intuits, that worries and bears the pain of helplessness. I need the sleep to rest my weary soul.

Before I began to walk with the immigrant and the poor, I had never put my face into the face of poverty for a sustained period of time. My journey with these young people is changing me. I am conscious that I now carry within me the story of many people oppressed by poverty. These are not the people who are half a world away—those whose bodies are more bone than flesh and whose sunken eyes are hauntingly captured on magazine covers—those for whom we pray with compassion while filled with gratitude for our own deliverance. The people who dwell in my heart live here in my own country. They are my neighbors. They shop at Wal-mart. While many view immigrants and their children as intruders, I have come to understand them as victims of economic displacement, a phenomenon that defies borders. While they may not appear half-starved, their lives are often so painfully poor that it is sometimes easier not to look in their direction.

Sometimes at Taller San Jose I have felt overwhelmed by the poverty that I see before me—the too-close living, the financial fear and insecurity, the hopelessness, the drug culture, and the crime-ridden neighborhoods. I've had to learn to keep my face in the face of human suffering, to stay focused and not to turn away when I've felt powerless to help. In his book, *Sabbath, Restoring the Sacred Rhythm of Rest,* Wayne Muller describes a conversation with an emergency room physician in a busy metropolis. The doctor hypothesizes that people at the front lines of medicine rush and hurry "because of the fear of the terrible things that they will feel in the quiet. They are so close to so much suffering and loss, they are afraid that if they stop, even for a moment, the sheer enormity of sorrow will suffocate and overwhelm them."[5] I think that is how it has been for me. I have often been horrified by the painful lives of the young people with whom I work. They are caught in the survival mode and cannot take the time to name their pain for fear it would paralyze them. I, on the other hand, absorb their pain and store their memories deep within me. Every day I keep these young people in my prayers. I want to surround them with the power and goodness of God—with courage, hope, perseverance, and the healing power of forgiveness. I know that tomorrow more young people will walk in the door, sharing new stories and laying out their brokenness and their needs. It is uncomfortable to be able to do so little in the face of so much human suffering.

And so I keep busy; I invent more tasks. I don't want to hear it all. Sometimes when I think that there is more room in my heart to store another sad story, I am wrong. And then, without warning, some trusting young person's tale of woe turns into sad, mad words that fill the room with heavy-winged moths. These dull gray creatures encircle me with their still soft darkness and beat at the door of my heart with their presence. But no more words can get in. Someone who looks just like me gets up and closes the shutters, double-bolts the doors, and seals all the airways that might lead to compassion. When my heart shuts down and I can hear no more, my car drives me home. A hot shower heals my outer core. But there is no one to soothe my soul just then. And so I seek the respite of time, the company of green trees, the imperceptible scent of day lilies, and the nirvana of a very long sleep. Only then do I go looking for the God who is with me at all times even when I do not see.

I've wondered at times if I will tire of my role here and of walking with these broken young people as they fumble their way between two cultures. Forward, backward, sideways, onward—they never take the route that I would choose for them. I suppose that every parent could say the same of their own children and that God could say the same of all his creatures. God could say the same of me.

CHAPTER SEVENTEEN

Somewhere there is a place waiting for me. Somehow I am going to get there.

—Juan Carrasco

People talk polite around nuns. Even though there's a good deal of prejudice expressed around and about me, I'm most often shielded from the worst of it. But I'm not blind to the fear and hostility about the burgeoning Mexican American population in California and the issue of immigration in my local environment.

The first time I heard the word *beaner,* it took me a beat or two to process the sting of its meaning and message. The loaded epithet came with the donation of a second-hand refrigerator to the convent. It had been a struggle to get the giant refrigerator in our front door to begin with. The donor had had to take the door off its hinges and with the help of a dolly he awkwardly maneuvered the refrigerator into the kitchen. Sweating and winded, he put the front door back in place, and when he was finished he headed for his truck. As he departed, I thanked him for his thoughtfulness, his time, and his trouble.

"Better you have it than some beaner," he quipped as he rolled up the car window and stepped on the gas.

Beaner? I'd never heard the word before, but it altogether sounded like *nigger* the way he had said it. I wanted to chase after him and push the refrigerator back upon him, but it was too late, he was around the corner and long gone. We were stuck with the cursed refrigerator for two years, and sometimes when I least expected, his biting words—*better you than some beaner,* cried out within me as I opened the door and reached for the milk.

I wonder how long you have to live in California before you're no longer considered a beaner? It's pretty clear to me that first- and second-generation immigrants are tagged beaners. But what if it was your grandparents who came from Mexico or your great-grandparents, or as was the case in my family that the border moved south and cut off one group of beaners from another over a hundred and fifty years ago?

Most borders are arbitrary boundaries meant to define political realities. Sometimes it's a river or a mountain range that separates one country from another. Then there are barriers like the Berlin Wall, built as a hostile reminder of the unfinished business of war and or the much-visited Great Wall of China, which served as a giant, cultural fence. Whatever their purpose or history, barriers and borders are meant to keep people in or keep people out. Although they're meant to establish geographical clarity and control the behavior of human transit, borders don't have much power over people's hearts—not if people want what's on the other side.

"Something there is that doesn't love a wall," says the poet Robert Frost, "that wants it down."[6] Across history and in geographies throughout the world, people have dug tunnels, skirted fences, and navigated rivers to cross a border if they believed that the key to their survival was on the other side.

I've crossed a number of international borders in my life but I've never crossed one that's the equal of the border between Tijuana, Mexico and San Ysidro, California. The border there is a mean-looking fence with high barbed wire that's angled southward at the top. It extends a good ways out into the ocean, daring the best of swimmers to challenge rough waters and uncertain tides. As the high foreboding blockade merges out from the land and into the sea it resembles the exterior of a colossal maximum security prison.

Nearly forty million people cross the San Ysidro border each year in cars, buses, and on foot. There's a free flow of traffic driving south from California and crossing into Mexico, but the return trip into the United States is tedious and can try frayed nerves. It's a long bumper-to-bumper wait behind long lines of cars as you inch your way toward the checkpoint. Twenty-four lanes mysteriously merge to eighteen at the crossing. Some drivers, convinced that fate condemns them to the slow lane, forge their way from one lane to the next using their vehicles like tanks and winning their modest victories by millimeters.

At the checkpoint, the border patrol officers talk to each passenger in every vehicle, verifying citizenship, asking the purpose of the visit, surveying the claimed purchases—all the while checking for drugs or contraband or for the possibility that a Mexican national might be hiding under a blanket on the floor of a vehicle or in the trunk or a car. The only distraction during the tedious wait time is the stream of vendors who walk between the lines of cars and hawk everything from pink, glitter-framed replicas of Leonardo da Vinci's *Last Supper* to bubble gum.

The real drama, though, is the sharp contrast in lifestyle, zoning, flora, and fauna between one country and the other. North of the border, in California, a mix of palm, pine, and eucalyptus trees line the wide freeways. Lush carpets of fuchsia ice plants flow down the terraced hillsides. Shopping malls and clean bright restaurants promise travelers comfort, cleanliness, and choice.

To the south, Tijuana is grimy and noisy. Dented and damaged older-model used cars are the norm on the crowded streets. If there are flowers or trees, they're all but hidden by the preponderance of concrete and the spikes of rebar jutting out of failed building projects. On the Mexican side of the border, young men perch on high ground where they can see above and beyond the tall spiked, steel wall that separates the two countries. In solitary vigil, they ponder what might await them on the other side.

Three thousand industries, mostly American, Japanese, and Korean companies have their factories—*maquiladoras*—on the

Mexican side of the border, taking advantage of the multitude of low-wage workers available. Jobs in the *maquiladora* sector and potential employment in the United States help attract continuing waves of migrants from central and southern Mexico, assuring the rapid growth of both Tijuana and its surrounding urban sprawl.

When you fly between the United States and Baja California, you can look down and see that the border is just an imaginary line, a human invention that separates the two disparate economies. Yet the line has power to change lives in dramatic ways.

Last year, Marta Mayorga, crossed from Tijuana to San Diego to have her second baby. Marta and her husband Guillermo are upper middle-class Mexicans. They both teach at a local university. Although they are Mexican and proud of it, they want their children to have the benefit of American citizenship as well—to have preferred futures with broad economic choices. And so Marta sought her prenatal care in San Diego. She and her husband prepaid for her medical costs in cash. The weekend before her delivery, she and Guillermo registered at a motel in San Diego and visited the local movie theatre where they viewed a marathon of films until her labor pains began. When the time between her contractions shortened, they drove to the preselected hospital where the physician in charge of her care attended the birth of her child.

The next day, with a new American citizen in tow, they drove south across the border into Tijuana—and home.

In Santa Ana, Miguel Martinez had an entirely different philosophy, born out of his macho, nationalistic pride. He wanted his children to be born in Mexico, and so when his wife, Xochil, was nearing the time of her delivery, he drove her across the border to his sister's house. There, with no prenatal care and no physician in attendance, she gave birth to each of their six children. And then they returned home—to Santa Ana, where

Miguel did landscaping and Xochil cared for her children and those of her extended family in their small, rented house. The Martinez children, faced a major hurdle though, when they came of age. Although they had been raised in California since infancy, none of these young people were American citizens. They could not get legal employment or obtain a driver's license and if they wanted to attend the local university, they had to pay out-of-state tuition fees.

It's true that there is enormous poverty in Mexico. There aren't a lot of jobs there at wages that permit people to support a family. But not everyone in Mexico is poor. There is industry and education and opportunity in Mexico and quite a number of Mexican citizens have either been able to live comfortably there and advance their economic position or at least to survive without great want. But the economy of Mexico simply doesn't support the burgeoning population of the country and the poverty there is historic and endemic. It's the poor and the hungry, not the middle-class Mexican, who sneaks across the border in the dark of night, risking his life and all of his life savings to do so.

Throughout California one now hears Spanish spoken in supermarkets, shopping malls, banks, theatres, and restaurants. Spanish advertisements paper the billboards and ride on the sides of buses. Spanish language television and radio continue to expand and they gobble up an ever-increasing share of the media market.

As the population of Mexican Americans and Mexican nationals in California grows, prejudice against the brown-skinned population of the state increases. Almost daily, there are articles in the newspapers decrying the preferential treatment given to the undocumented and calling for the deportation of Mexicans.

In 1986, when Congress passed the Immigration Reform and Control Act, the intent was to close the back door of illegal immigration and to grant amnesty to individuals who could prove continuous residency in the United States since 1982. At the same time, legal sanctions were enacted against employers, imposing fines and other penalties for hiring undocumented workers. In actuality, the program failed. The nearly three million people who applied for amnesty created a log jam for the immigration system which continues to this day. Moreover, relying chiefly on voluntary compliance, employer sanctions failed. Meanwhile the rapid expansion of service industries, the fast food industries, and the competition of global industries created a demand for more and more low-income workers. Hardly anyone agrees that maintaining a large, permanent, illegal population is good for the country or even for the individuals themselves. Undocumented immigrants can be easily victimized by employers and landlords. Even a fellow countryman can take advantage of the new immigrant, sometimes setting up scams and charging the unwary exorbitant fees while not delivering promised services.

The 2000 Census revealed that there are between 4.4 and 5 million unauthorized immigrants living in the United States. By 2030, California is predicted to become a minority/majority state—a geography in which the Latino population predominates. In the first decade of the twenty-first century, the state economy is crumbling from the burden of providing medical care, education, police protection, and a prison system to house nonlegal residents. Everyday, the newspaper carries one story or another or a letter to the editor about the dilemma and conflicts of absorbing a large illegal immigrant population. Arguments are posited, pro and con, on the subject, the vast majority being opposed to the massive influx of people from south of the border even though many believe that the economy probably benefits from immigration.

California has a love/hate relationship with Mexico and Mexicans. We've learned to make guacamole and tacos. We can blend a mean Margarita and we hire mariachis for our weddings and piñatas often replace pin-the-tail-on-the-donkey at children's birthday parties. Our economy is dependent upon a continuous stream of cheap labor from south of the border, whether legal or illegal. Often we do not ask.

Mexicans and Mexican Americans are the gardeners, the busboys, the dishwashers, the cleaning ladies, and the nannies that make comfort and convenience affordable. It would be unthinkable to abolish this vast, largely unskilled labor force. The under class makes the upper class possible.

Still, a number of Californians would like the Mexicans to go home and sometimes there is little differentiation about who should go home—those born in Mexico or those born in the United States to immigrants from Mexico or those born here a generation ago. It's all so confusing; they may look and sound pretty much the same. And where exactly should they go and when? "Down on brown" is an attitude that floats freely throughout California and often there is little differentiation upon whom it lands. It's hardly an invitation to successful acculturation.

Many present day Americans, who have roots in Western Europe, now proudly share stories of how and why their ancestors came in time of trouble, war, or famine. Their separation from their country of origin, their culture, and their families was not an option. It was the forced choice of economic survival. They wanted to live and to give life to their children. These immigrants of the nineteenth and early twentieth centuries hit the land hard and scrappy. Some ran; some fell; others stumbled along the way. Now we point pridefully to their photos and share the story scraps of their lives while we stand on their shoulders and cling to the American dream. History invites nostalgia.

Yet today's immigrant experience is quite different from that of a century ago. There's not as much land for one thing, or water, or resources for healthcare and education. Even parking spaces are harder to come by. There are more guns and gangs and drugs to contend with and the streets of our cities are meaner. Violence is more widespread, frequent, and unpredictable. In the midst of a world war on terrorism that we can barely name and that we prayed would never come, we demand the right to control our borders and to determine who is friend and who is foe. There are decisions to be made. So who goes and who stays and in whom do we invest for the future?

I was raised on a Gospel that proclaims that every life is precious from conception until death. I believe the same more strongly each day. I don't know why I was called upon to care about these particular young men and women in Santa Ana, those caught in the deluge of poverty and instability, but I do care about them deeply.

They are young, most in their late teens and early twenties. They didn't ask for the challenge of being caught between two cultures or the snare of crushing poverty, and they have fallen between the cracks too soon while struggling to find a foothold in life.

Some of their brothers, cousins, and friends have already been gunned down in gang fights; some have begun to walk a path that will lead to perpetual imprisonment; still others are just scared, lost, and stuck, sitting on couches in crowded apartments waiting for life to happen.

As I've met these young people, in their woes, I've wanted to remove from them the burden of poverty and its ugly consequences. In one grand, sweeping motion, I've longed to lift them above misery and set them down in a valley of plenty. But this is not within my power and even if I could ransom one and then another in this way, every day more young people walk through the door. I cannot make their lives as carefree and privileged as mine has been though I hope they have more strength and dignity because of Taller San Jose, and I believe that they have the ability to make a better life for their children. In this brief point of contact, if I try to soften their lives and shield them from life's challenges, I take away their ability to build the strength that they will need for their journey.

I view myself as a realist informed by the Gospel. I don't know how to solve the complexities of the immigration crisis or the chaos of desperation that emerges when the poverty of Mexico butts up against the affluence of the United States. I do know that when day after day people from Mexico and Central America risk their lives on journeys through cold mountain passes, the blistering heat of deserts, or in the back of unventilated trucks, that they are not seeking "the good life" for they have never seen it. They are desperately clinging to a hope that they may have life at all and that one day they might help their children rise out of poverty.

Whatever the challenges and arguments about this current wave of immigration and its effect upon American society, I've seen too much now. It is no longer possible for me to turn away from the young people who inhabit my day-to-day world for I know that if I shut them out of my waking hours, they will surely visit me in my dreams. Their stories and their struggles are forever tattooed upon my heart.

They don't deserve to live in darkness. I believe that we fail ourselves and our society if we label our young "dropouts, messups, and felons," let them lie in the gutter of life, and turn our faces away as we pass by. Some time when we are not looking, they will struggle to their feet and they will soldier on—somehow, and their children after them will do the same. I wonder, will it be in the dark or the daylight?

A FINAL CHAPTER

Never worry about numbers. Help one person at a time, and always start with the person nearest you.
—Mother Teresa

Mother Teresa of Calcutta and I were both invited to speak at the National Catholic Education Convention in 1975. The convention was held in the spring in Chicago. I spoke to a group of about three hundred people. I can barely remember the topic—something related to the public relations issues of Catholic schools. I was thirty-five years old, flattered to have been selected as a speaker, and quite nervous.

I no longer wore a religious habit, but I had chosen my clothes for the occasion carefully, a tailored navy blue dress to which I fixed my small wooden cross—the image of the polished, professional American nun. On the morning of the scheduled event, I checked out my appearance in the full-length mirror in my hotel room and reviewed my notes one last time before I left for the convention center. I made it through the presentation well enough, I suppose, but when it was over, I was relieved to have the thing behind me.

Later that day Mother Teresa spoke to a crowd of ten thousand in the arena of the convention center. When she came out onto the stage, the entire audience rose in unison and then there followed a lengthy applause that no one was willing to break.

Mother Teresa was a diminutive woman. Alone, in front of a backdrop of deep gold velvet curtains, she appeared as David before the Goliath of the world's ills. She was sixty-six years old at the time and already she was stooped from decades of hard work. Her face wore the deep furrows of compassion that we later came to view as trophies of a graced life. While the crowd in the arena applauded her, she stood with quiet dignity, her hands raised slightly at her sides. From time to time, she nodded her head in the most humble manner to acknowledge the recognition.

This tribute isn't for me, she indicated by her simple self-effacing posture, *I let the praise pass through me to the God who uses me as His instrument.*

As the accolade continued, I felt warm tears course down my face. I am certain that I was not alone in my emotional response to the power of grace and goodness that this humble woman witnessed.

Mother Teresa didn't need a podium when she spoke because she didn't use any notes. I feel quite sure that she hadn't checked out her white and blue Indian sari in the mirror before leaving her hotel room. When she stood before the immense crowd, she spoke from her heart what she knew to be the truth. I didn't take any notes that day but I wanted to remember what she said, and so I must have scribbled her words upon my heart. Although I can no longer quote her word for word, her simple, direct message was one, that in essence, she preached throughout her life. The straightforward clarity of her conviction reminded us that the knowledge of these simple truths rests within every human heart.

- *Every human being was created by God and is deserving of dignity and respect.*

- *Every human life is precious.*

- *No human creature is superior to another because of culture, possession of resources, education, or fortuitous circumstances.*

- *The poor deserve our utmost respect and concern.*

- *We who have are obliged to share with those who suffer want.*

We had all stood for her, I think, because she unashamedly stood for the poorest of the poor, those people who were cast into the gutter to die. It is possible to ignore human suffering or even to take a life if one can define the other as subhuman, inferior to oneself. But that day Mother Teresa lifted the poor and dying out of the gutter and set them before us, inviting us all to see the poor through her eyes.

When Mother Teresa spoke about the conditions in India's poorest cities and about how people without resources or family were left in the streets to die in filth, she cautioned us against rushing off to India to help her. She explained that while many people who heard of the good works of the Missionaries of Charity were eager to join them in Calcutta and to work alongside them, she strongly advised against this. The culture of India was very different from our own, she said, and it was quite possible that God was not asking us to radically change our cultures and to leave our families in order to help the poor. Rather, she invited us to look in our own backyards for opportunities to serve those most in need.

She reminded us that the poor are all around us. That they are, in fact, everywhere. God did not mean for us all to move to India, she cautioned again, and then she issued a strong invitation to us to become as involved in our own neighborhoods and cities as she was on the streets of Calcutta. She told us to draw a circle around our lives and to notice if there was anyone near to us who needed our help.

"Always start with the person nearest to you first," she said. Then she asked us to draw ever larger concentric circles around our lives, searching in each one of them until we found those less fortunate than ourselves with whom we could share our time, our talent, or our treasure.

Mother Teresa ended her simple, focused message with the reminder that God loves us all equally, but that He has a special concern for the poorest of the poor.

Everyone in the arena that day, people of every faith and culture, knew that what she was doing was right—directing all of her energy to the most neglected people of the world.

We stood for her that day because she stood for the dignity of the human person and it ennobled us to be in her presence.

⊱✦⊰

Several years later I had an opportunity to draw a bigger circle around my life and to respond to the need that I saw before me—the young people who were killing each other or else dying from within on the streets of my city.

I have never been alone in my circle of concern.

Every year at Taller San Jose we work directly and personally with over five hundred young people. We walk with them through drug addictions, court hearings, the tedious earning of credits toward a high school diploma, their health concerns, jail time, childbirth, and the reordering of life at the end of painful relationships. We celebrate every achievement—the acquiring of a driver's license, the opening of a bank account, the first day on a job, certification of a skill and the earning of a diploma, a raise in salary.

It takes a decent wage to rise out of poverty, but you can't earn a living wage without confident, concrete skills. That's why walking young people out of poverty—all the way out—requires a significant investment of personal and financial resources.

All around me each day, generous and caring people give of themselves to provide the young people of Santa Ana a fighting chance at life. A talented staff, armed with wisdom and compassion, pours out its energies to create a system of seamless support. A steady stream of volunteers tutors students in the basics of math and language arts—essentials that time has erased within them. An active board of directors shepherds the project and connects it to the wealth of resources in the surrounding community. Each year a cadre of imaginative women sponsor a fundraiser that nets over $300,000 in program support. Builders, developers, and employers provide materials and services and stand ready to hire young people as they emerge from training programs.

In spite of many barriers and setbacks, the majority of Taller San Jose's students advance one uncertain step at a time. Forty-six percent of students eventually achieve their high school diplomas, many moving on to community college. Seventy-three percent of Taller San Jose's graduates find employment beyond minimum wage, and best of all, of those who have been previously incarcerated, 97 percent are not rearrested for violent crime.

And God in heaven watches over these precious young sparrows until they fly...until they fly...

EPILOGUE

A rush of adrenaline gives to my fists strength to continue the fight against my odds.

—Juan Carrasco

In these pages, I've shared the stories of only a few of Taller San Jose's students. Their lives and their stories touched me because in their responses to the obstacles that they faced, these young people have exemplified the most common responses to life's challenges—courage, bewilderment, perseverance, dogged determination, and disappointment. For every young person who fails to successfully negotiate the barriers of poverty in crime-infested neighborhoods, countless others *do* succeed.

When they succeed, it is because a parent, a teacher, a counselor, a church worker, a coach, or an employer has believed in them and walked with them through the rough patches of life. Like many others who reach out to these young people, I have come to understand that it is not one's brilliance, energy or competence that makes a difference in their lives, rather it is a steady and sometimes helpless presence that counts and the knowledge that we are, after all, companions on the same human journey.

To the best of my knowledge, this is where these young people are today.

Armando Ibarra, who had haltingly recounted the accusation of rape to me in our convent parlor, was ultimately cleared of the charges against him. He complied with the court mandate to attend AA meetings and graduated from Taller San Jose with his high school diploma. His friend, **Javier Ponce,** who accompanied him that evening, dropped out of school and now works with his father.

Ramon Padilla has completed a computer training program and has steady, full-time employment for the first time in his life. He has continued to stay clean and sober.

The last time I heard from **Yolanda Castro** she called me from a pay phone to ask my help in finding her a drug treatment program. I made a connection for her but she never called back. Yolanda's daughter is being cared for by her sister.

Eddie Vargas, a former Taller San Jose woodworker, is employed as a cabinet maker. His two felonies and the incomplete status of his documentation in the United States caused him to live in fear of deportation during the time he spent at Taller San Jose. With his subsequent track record as a steady worker and provider and because of his long-term crime free behavior, Eddie has recently been granted permanent resident status and he will work toward achieving his citizenship as soon as he qualifies. A Taller San Jose staff member testified in his behalf at the immigration hearing. Eddie and his wife have three children, all of whom are American citizens. His brother, **Omar,** credits Taller San Jose with helping him to stay out of trouble during the critical years of his adolescence. Omar, who came to this country when he was a year old, has also been granted legal status in the United States and now has the ability to support his wife and children with the promise of stable employment. His current goals are to apply for citizenship and to study to become a police officer.

Luis Peralta has recovered from his gunshot wounds. The metal rods inserted into his fingers have fused successfully with his bones and he has limited use of his hand. Because of the fact that he is unskilled and now has a disability, Luis has had difficulty finding steady work. Frieda, his woman and the mother of his second son, is the primary bread-winner for the family. He remains close to his sons.

Marisol Duran works in a neighborhood convenience store. Her four boys are now fifteen, twelve, eleven, and seven. She has returned to Taller San Jose for the second time to try to complete her high school diploma. The father of her children still cycles in and out of prison.

Mario Pineda works a double-shift as a nursing assistant. He now earns $9.50 an hour and is struggling to support himself, his wife, and his baby. The majority of his salary goes to pay the $975 per month rent on their modest one bedroom apartment.

Mona Gomez earns $12.00 an hour working as a nurse's aide in the oncology ward of the local Catholic hospital. Her daughter, Vanessa, is five years old. Ivan, Vanessa's father, still hovers in the background. Mona is determined to advance to her RN degree.

Ruben Maldonado tested dirty for drug use after 110 days of treatment. He was dismissed from the drug treatment program and returned to his family's Santa Ana apartment. He works two jobs to support himself. He goes to Narcotics Anonymous meetings regularly and keeps a link with Taller San Jose.

Ricardo Perez, who left the program rather than participate in a drug treatment program, ultimately did return to Taller San Jose to finish high school. When he graduated he transferred to Taller San Jose Tech, entered the construction training program, and completed his certification in carpentry. Ricardo has stayed clean and sober for three years. He completed the previous terms of his probation and has not been rearrested. He now earns $15.40 an hour as an apprentice carpenter.

NOTES

1. Fulton Oursler and Will Oursler, *Father Flanagan of Boys Town* (Garden City, NY: Doubleday and Company, Inc., 1959), p. 113.).

2. John Henry Newman, "Hope in God—Creator," found in his collection *Meditations and Devotions*. Newman's works, biographical information, and details about his cause for sainthood can be found on the Newman Reader Web site at www.newmanreader.org.

3. Mary Lou Kownacki, OSB, *The Blue Heron and Thirty-Seven Other Miracles* (Erie, Pa: Benetvision, 1999), p. 60.

4. Henri Nouwen, *Return of the Prodigal Son* (New York: Doubleday, 1994).

5. Wayne Mueller, *Sabbath: Restoring the Sacred Rhythm of Rest* (New York: Bantam, 1999), p. 52.

6. Robert Frost, *The Poetry of Robert Frost: The Collected Poems, Prose, and Plays* (New York: Library Classics of the United States, Inc., 1995), p. 39.